AMERICAN POETS PROJECT

AMERICAN POETS PROJECT

IS PUBLISHED WITH A GIFT IN MEMORY OF

James Merrill

AND SUPPORT FROM ITS FOUNDING PATRONS

Sidney J. Weinberg, Jr. Foundation

The Berkley Foundation

Richard B. Fisher and Jeanne Donovan Fisher

Amy Lowell

selected poems

honor moore editor

AMERICAN POETS PROJECT

THE LIBRARY OF AMERICA

Design by Chip Kidd and Mark Melnick.
Frontispiece: By permission of the Houghton Library, Harvard University; Bachrach, Inc., "Amy Lowell Photographs"

Library of Congress Cataloging-in-Publication Data:
Lowell, Amy, 1874–1925.
    [Poems. Selections]
    Selected poems / Amy Lowell; Honor Moore, editor.
        p. cm. — (American poets project ; 12)
    Includes biographical references and index.
    ISBN 1–931082–70–7 (alk. paper)
        I. Moore, Honor, 1945–. II. Title. III. Series.
PS3523.O88A6 2004
821'.912 — dc22
200404805

10 9 8 7 6 5 4 3 2 1

Amy
Lowell

CONTENTS

Posthumously Published Poems

INTRODUCTION

To utter the name Amy Lowell is to enter the fraught literary wars of early Modernism. Almost immediately, we see an extremely short, extremely stout woman arguing forcefully with a young man with frizzy reddish hair and a goatee. The pince-nez on the woman's delicate nose looks tiny because her face is so enormous, and the young man is dressed in a velvet jacket; "never, since the days of Wilde, have such garments been seen in the streets of London," the woman will later report. At first Amy Lowell and Ezra Pound admire each other and then they hate each other, leaving paper trails to prove it. *Amygism!* someone shouts, baiting with Pound's vengeful epithet. To hear his partisans tell it, the principles of Imagism were Pound's genius and Amy Lowell appropriated, even stole, them. In fact, the British poet T. E. Hulme first conceived the ideas, and Pound, ever restless, abandoned Imagism for Vorticism as soon as he issued *Des Imagistes* (1914), an anthology published in London of six poets including himself,

H.D., Richard Aldington, William Carlos Williams, and Amy Lowell.

What caused the ruckus was that Lowell, inspired to bring the Imagists into print in America, edited three more anthologies, one each in 1915, 1916, and 1917, in which Pound refused to be included. He'd selected and blue-penciled the poems in his collection, but Lowell invited contributors to choose their own and meticulously split the royalties. "Democratized," Pound sneered. "Thank you so much for the cheque for £8, which came today," wrote D. H. Lawrence to Lowell in 1916. "Those Imagiste books seem to blossom into gold like a monthly rose."

Lawrence, who composed *Women in Love* on a typewriter Lowell gave him, became a lifelong friend, as did Robert Frost and Thomas Hardy, but we are never told the facts of Amy Lowell's literary life. "And she smoked cigars!" Yes, she did, notably one night on shipboard years before proper women did so in public. She refused a society interview on landing in New York, the indignant journalist found a witness, and the next morning front pages all over America proclaimed that the sister of the president of Harvard smoked "big black" cigars.

Actually, Lowell was a delicate woman and her cigars were slender Manilas. Before long, her notoriety would come from her vocal defense of "the new poetry," not from what she inhaled, and her fame from her writing rather than who her brother was—her posthumous collection *What's O'Clock* won the Pulitzer for poetry in 1926, and her books, including her poetry collections, routinely reached best-seller lists. At the height of her career, Lowell was spending weeks each year touring, performing her poems to packed halls and lecturing to hundreds. Young poets gathered at her feet, rapt as she held forth—Carl Sandburg likened the effect of her company to "a bright blue wave." She also had a wicked sense of humor. Unwrapping one of her Manilas was like undressing a lady, she told one young man. First you remove the belt (the first cigar band), then the evening dress (the silver paper wrapping), the slip (a square of tissue paper), and finally the girdle (the second cigar band).

But what are her poems like? Anyone with more than a passing knowledge of American poetry has heard of Amy Lowell, but few have read more than one poem, usually the widely anthologized "Patterns," written at the onset of World War I. The speaker, in her "stiff, brocaded gown," contemplates the rarified patterning of her garden and declares with distaste that, with her "powdered hair and jewelled fan," she herself is no more than a "rare pattern,"—

> Not a softness anywhere about me,
> Only whalebone and brocade.
> And I sink on a seat in the shade
> Of a lime tree. For my passion
> Wars against the stiff brocade.

She thinks of her fiancé, fantasizes she has led him through the maze-like flowerbeds until "the buttons of his waistcoat bruised my body as he clasped me, / Aching, melting, unafraid." But the footman has brought a message—her lover has died in battle; she will never break the pattern, is destined to be forever

> . . . guarded from embrace
> By each button, hook, and lace.
> For the man who should loose me is dead,
> Fighting with the Duke in Flanders,
> In a pattern called a war.
> Christ! What are patterns for?

Christ! What are patterns for? a woman friend recited back when I mentioned Amy Lowell. "That poem was so important to me . . . " Though "Patterns" situates female sexual desire in opposition to patriarchal strictures like bones and stays, formal gardens and war, what strikes the contemporary reader is not the sophistication of Lowell's feminist and antiwar stances, but the bald audacity of her eroticism. "Underneath my stiffened gown / Is the softness of a woman bathing in a marble basin," the speaker says. She would like to see her brocaded gown "lying in a heap upon the ground / All the pink and silver crumpled up . . . " and further, "I would be the pink and silver as I ran along the paths, /And he would stumble after . . . "

To read through *The Complete Poetical Works of Amy Lowell*, edited by Louis Untermeyer in the 1950s, is to become aware that her most significant poetic achievement lies not in free verse narratives like "Patterns," but in the erotic lyrics she wrote to the woman with whom she lived the final twelve years of her life. Here is "The Weather-Cock Points South," first published in *Vanity Fair* in 1919:

> I put your leaves aside,
> One by one:
> The stiff, broad outer leaves;
> The smaller ones,
> Pleasant to touch, veined with purple;
> The glazed inner leaves.
> One by one
> I parted you from your leaves,
> Until you stood up like a white flower
> Swaying slightly in the evening wind.
>
> White flower,
> Flower of wax, of jade, of unstreaked agate;

Flower with surfaces of ice,
With shadows faintly crimson.
Where in all the garden is there such a flower?
The stars crowd through the lilac leaves
To look at you.
The low moon brightens you with silver.

The bud is more than the calyx.
There is nothing to equal a white bud,
Of no colour, and of all,
Burnished by moonlight,
Thrust upon by a softly-swinging wind.

All of Amy Lowell's influences are present in this poem. She was just beginning to read the Chinese poets of the T'ang Dynasty, and we can feel in her restraint the affinity that would draw her later to translate Li Po and Tu Fu. But what propels "The Weather-Cock . . . " is hardly restraint, nor does the poem turn on an irony as classical Chinese poems often do. Instead, the speaker's focused intention moves the poem, constructing images from imagination rather than observation—"Flower of wax, of jade, of unstreaked agate; / Flower with surfaces of ice, / With shadows faintly crimson."—emulating the painterliness the poet admired in de Regnier, de Gourmont, and particularly Verhaeren, French pre-Modernists important to Lowell and her contemporaries for the seriousness with which they made a poetry free of *l'ancien rite* of French metrical tradition.

But just as we are lulled by artifice, Lowell shifts to engaged observation that recalls the Keats she adored— "The stars crowd through the lilac leaves / To look at you. / The low moon brightens you with silver." The French pre-Modernists wrote a *vers libre* that was musical and often dramatic, while the Imagists, breaking with English

Romantic tradition, aspired to a poetry more like the Greek lyric—as Lowell put it, "hard and clear, never blurred nor indefinite." In "The Weather-Cock Points South," Lowell does both.

Her Greek was Sappho, whom she likened, in a poem called "The Sisters," to "a burning birch-tree / All tall and glittering fire." Reading Amy Lowell as a woman of her time and place, one can see why. The persona of "Patterns" recalls women then being painted by William Paxton and Edward Tarbell, Boston School artists who placed solitary female subjects in elegant, patterned surroundings to await, if not the sexual agency of a man, a force to carry them into life. Even in poems like "The Pike," in which no "I" is present, Lowell's lyrics disrupt that pattern, offering an unmediated, active female speaker. In "The Weather-Cock . . . " she goes further, inviting us to read her "I" as the poet herself enacting imaged homoerotic love-making: "I put your leaves aside, /one by one: / The stiff, broad outer leaves; / The smaller ones . . . / veined with purple . . . " Here is writing that resonates not only with Imagism and the French pre-Moderns, but with the silky Paris Sapphism of Natalie Barney, the American emigrée and saloniere who entertained Proust on the rue Jacob, seduced the courtesan Liane de Pougy, and, with her lover, the pseudonymous Renée Vivian, translated Sappho's fragments, unearthed in abundance for the first time in the 1890s.

Amy Lowell never escaped to Paris or even New York. She traveled, but always returned to Boston, where, as a Brahmin Lowell, she was allowed any behavior as long as it wasn't spoken of. Her erotic life remained within the confines of the family estate in Brookline, where she lived her entire life, and within poems rendered discreet by titles like "The Weather-Cock Points South" or "The Blue Scarf." In public manner, she followed the example of wealthy Boston women of a generation before her who chose activism over despondent idleness—Elizabeth Peabody, who revolutionized children's education, Pauline Agassiz Shaw, who financed settlement houses, and the Massachusetts suffragist Lucy Stone. Their examples would inspire Boston women of later generations to turn mind-deadening debutante society clubs into vehicles for the emancipation and recruitment to social work of young women of privilege.

Given this context, it is no wonder that Lowell framed her personal literary quest as a campaign—she saw and spoke of "the new poetry" as "our cause." And she suffered the consequences. Like many powerful unmarried women in public life, Amy Lowell was ridiculed, and like all effective crusaders, she had adversaries. Ezra Pound's account of her, epitomized by his epithet, Amygisme, has survived to curse her integrity and obscure her poetic accomplishment. Even her great friend the critic Louis Untermeyer covered his bets. In his subtitle of her posthumous complete poems, Lowell is "A Militant Crusader for Modern Poetry," as if she had been a polemicist rather than a poet who produced, during a thirteen-year career, ten books of poems, a collection of Chinese translations, three books of literary essays, a two-volume biography of Keats, and countless occasional pieces.

Though her lyrics are her most distinctive work, Lowell experimented with free verse that she called "cadenced verse" and pioneered the prose poem in English. In "polyphonic prose," she undertook prose poem epics about Napoleon and Josephine and Lord Nelson and Emma Hamilton, and in cadenced verse she wrote narrative poems in New England dialect and, after spending the first months of World War I stranded in Paris, a group of anti-war poems. Her Brahmin pedigree required a split between public and private: her public poems she famously performed, while her lyrics, it seems, were kept safe and quiet on the page.

Amy Lowell was born in 1874 into a family, her biographer, the Blake scholar Foster Damon, wrote, "composed of individuals who were astonishingly indifferent to the opinions of others, who were much given to public benefactions and public controversies, and who tended to be manufacturers, judges, poets, scholars and critics, and horticulturalists." This inheritance enabled her two sisters to marry well and her brother Lawrence to become the innovative president of Harvard who instituted its tutorial system. Her favorite brother, Percival, a writer whose books about his decade in Japan and China inspired Lafcadio Hearn to travel to the Far East, was later an astronomer who built the Lowell Observatory in Arizona in order to observe Mars (he wrote a controversial book about its "canals") and had a part in the intellectual work that led to the discovery of Pluto. Amy was the youngest by eleven years and, because her mother was confined to bed with Bright's disease, she became a solitary child, a tomboy dreamer who spent hours alone at Sevenels, the Brookline estate her father, the textile manufacturer Augustus Lowell, built and named for the seven "L's" who lived there.

Possessed of too searching and disruptive an intelligence for the casual instruction Boston offered daughters of the rich, Amy left school at sixteen and resumed her education on her own, beginning in her father's library and continuing in the spiral-staired stacks of the Boston Atheneum, of which her great-grandfather John Lowell III had been a founder. Out of those years of reading came the revelation that existence could be engaged through literature and art. Amy was aware of poetry as a child, having been "hauled into the library" to meet her father's famous cousin, the poet James Russell Lowell: "I was afraid of his grandeur and his reticence, and he considered me a poor little girl whom he had to speak to." But aside from the ordinary experiments of childhood, she did not begin to write poems until she was twenty-eight, a dozen years after an epiphany brought on by reading Leigh Hunt's *Imagination and Fancy*. "I did not read it," she wrote, "I devoured it. I read it over and over, and then I turned to the works of the poets referred to, and tried to read them by the light of the new aesthetic perception I had learnt from Hunt . . . "

Her excitement was so great she "used to inveigle my schoolmates up to my room and read them long stretches of Shelley, and Keats, and Coleridge, and Beaumont and Fletcher." She bemoaned the poverty of her formal education. "Guided by Hunt I found a new Shakespeare, one of whom I had never dreamed . . . the plays were saved for me." It was Keats, though, who became her great mentor. She understood his landscape, having wandered, mesmerized, through her father's gardens. His certainty "of nothing but the holiness of the heart's affections and the truth of the imagination" enabled her to see her solitude as a resource, and reading of the lovers in *Endymion* gave her an understanding of the spiritual dimension in physical love and a belief that language could safely express sexual yearning. Eventually, she would assemble the largest collection of Keats manuscripts then in private hands, raise money for the preservation of his residences in Rome and Hampstead, and, late in life, write his first major American biography.

●

But Keats could not rescue Amy Lowell from enacting the rites of passage expected of a Lowell daughter. Though she was five foot one and, even her friends remarked, "almost as wide," she applied herself at Mr. Papanti's dancing school; when she made her debut in 1891 her dance card was always full. She was light on her feet and a vivacious conversationalist who took easily to the Boston sport of repartee, which belied Gertrude Stein's bromide that "remarks are not literature." "Good Americans when they die go to Paris," Tom Appleton had famously quipped a half century earlier, equally famously christening his home city "cold roast Boston." It was Amy Lowell's good fortune that in the 1890s the roast on the Charles River was absorbing a decidedly fin de siecle marinade—the decor was Arts and Crafts, the writers were Huysmans, Laforgue, and, via Stone and Kimball's *Chap Book*, Verlaine, Maeterlinck and Mallarmé.

At salons and musicales devised by "Mrs. Whitman" and "Mrs. Gardner," conversation transcended repartee, and the hostesses were formidable arbiters of taste. The painter Sarah Wyman Whitman had studied in France with Thomas Couture and in Boston with William Morris Hunt, and her circle included Sarah Orne Jewett and Charles Eliot Norton, with whom she had been a founder of the Boston Society of Arts and Crafts. When Lowell knew her, Whitman was designing books for Houghton Mifflin, producing stained glass windows commissioned by the likes of Harvard and Trinity Church, and bringing together the artistic young in her Beacon Street parlor. Across town, Isabella Stewart Gardner held musicales in the "Tapestry Room" of the Italianate villa she'd built on the Fenway, perennially attracting rumors of sensual excess: she lined a room with black velvet or posed nude for a group of gentlemen artists. She repented a transgression by scrubbing the steps of the Episcopal Church of the Advent on Good Friday. Gardner was also assembling the art collection she opened to the public in 1903, the greatest and most serious of its time, and entertaining guests like Henry James and her sometime lover, the novelist Francis Marion Crawford.

As these women offered Lowell glimpses of unconventionality, she watched her friends, one after another, marry and leave behind the post-debut round of luncheons and house parties. As time went on, Amy herself turned aside two offers of marriage, but in 1897, when an unnamed Bostonian proposed, she overcame her resistance and actually fell in love with him. Her father approved the match and the engagement was all but announced when the young man broke it off. Eventually, the failed engagement would allow Lowell, without the risk of censure, to free herself of society's requirements, but in its immediate aftermath, devastated and humiliated, she took to her bed and shut the door. When she emerged, she resolved to make herself marriageable, taking a three-month cruise up the Nile with two friends, a chaperone, and a maid. The aim was weight loss; the method, Egyptian heat and Dr. Willard Banting's fashionable diet of asparagus and tomatoes. But "banting" and slenderness had no place in Amy's letters home to her father, which articulate astonishments that even now engage the reader with the sensual charge that made her a poet: "Never shall I forget Abo Simbel as our dahabeah swung around the curve in the river and there four colossal figures sat gazing down upon the blue river with that bright orange tumble of sand beside them." Banting's diet broke Lowell's health and she suffered the consequences for years, but after Egypt, she accepted her body and her situation. Her overweight was due to a glandular disorder that was incurable. At twenty-four, Amy

Lowell did not yet know what she would do, but she was not destined to become a Boston matron.

Before the Egyptian journey, Katharine Lowell had succumbed to Bright's disease, and, as was expected of a spinster daughter, Amy became her widowed father's hostess. Two years after Egypt, when Augustus Lowell suddenly died, Amy, now twenty-six, was faced with making a life on her own. To that end, she purchased Sevenels from her siblings and, as was expected of a Lowell, volunteered for public duties in Brookline. She brought all her formidable energy to these projects, even chairing something called the Committee for the Suppression of Unnecessary Noise. Eventually her forcefulness clashed with the expectations of others. When she gave a public lecture criticizing the Brookline high school curriculum as "prejudicial to individual development," her Lowell aunts were appalled —women should not to speak publicly, let alone provoke controversy.

But Amy Lowell had been offered none of womanhood's compensations; why should she endure its proscriptions? She traveled, she fell in love with Naples and Venice, she marveled at Greece; in London, she collected rare books, bought Keats manuscripts, met Whistler and purchased one of his paintings. At Sevenels, she presented evenings of Debussy, Satie, Bartók, and George Antheil, and later started a little theater company in which she occasionally acted. Her greatest "handicap," she wrote later, was being "from a class that was not supposed to be able to produce creative work." In her twenties, she was doing just what artistic women of that class did—getting as close to the flame as possible without burning herself.

Flames burst the firewall one October evening in 1902. Lowell had seen Eleonora Duse twice, but neither experience prepared her for the actress's opening that autumn night at the new Tremont Theatre. Duse performed *La Gioconda* and *La Città Morta*, plays written for her by Gabriele d'Annunzio, who had left her and exposed their affair in a novel. "I went to see her," Amy wrote, "as I always went to see everything that was good in the theatre. The effect on me was something tremendous. What really happened was that it revealed me to myself, but I hardly knew that at the time. I just knew that I had got to express the sensations that Duse's acting gave me, somehow . . . "

Returning in great agitation to Sevenels, Amy sat up all night writing. The resulting poem (published in *Poetry* twenty years later as juvenilia, and not to be confused with the later poem of the same title in this volume) was, as Lowell herself commented, beginner's work. But in writing it, she not only touched the flame, she viscerally understood it was her destiny to embrace it. "I knew nothing whatever about the technique of poetry, and the poem is full of poeticisms and sappy rhetoric, but it is sincere. . . . " It also predicted Lowell's own creative aspiration—to yield to something real, beyond the material world:

> For she whom we have come to see tonight
> Is more to be divined and felt than seen,
> And when she comes one yields one's heart perforce,
> As one might yield some noble instrument. . . .
>
> And as the evening lengthens, bit by bit,
> Little by little, we discern the real. . . .

In the months that followed, as the riches of reading, travel, and experience began to fall together in poems, Amy's involvement in town committees, musicales, and amateur theatricals fell away. When she understood she wanted to write seriously, she joined her friend Elizabeth

Ward, also an aspiring poet, for study, returning to Leigh Hunt and Keats, writing poem after practice poem, pledging not to publish until the work was worthy. After eight years of effort, a sonnet called "A Fixed Idea" was taken by *The Atlantic*; several more magazine publications followed until, in 1912, Lowell's first collection was accepted by Houghton Mifflin. She was thirty-eight.

A Dome of Many-Coloured Glass received mostly respectful reviews, but it sold only modestly. Reading through it, one often feels the poet struggling with the burden of a poetic past while the woman chides herself for falling short of a womanly ideal, moralizing like her forbears who stitched samplers: "Chasten my steps to peaceful regularity," reads a line of "Fatigue," while in "A Fixed Idea" the poet assures us that "all recurring joy is pain refined, / Become a habit . . ." Once in a while though, a poem that begins aphoristically, like "The Starling"— "Forever the impenetrable wall / Of self confines my poor rebellious soul,"—concludes with an intimation of the poet's vulnerability and ambition: "I weary for dreams never guessed, / For alien passions, strange imaginings, / To be some other person for a day."

Who was this other person Lowell wished to become? For eight years she had worked and studied to become a poet; now she had published a book. But she understood there was an element missing. What would enable her to break through the "impenetrable wall" that kept her from deeper engagement with both poetry and experience? A convergence of events opened the way forward. In 1913, in *Poetry*, Lowell read the poems of H.D. The effect of Imagism on her poems was immediate, "brooming away Victorian cobwebs; reducing morals to implications," Foster Damon wrote, leading her to the French pre-Modernists. Barely a year later, reading the first unbowdlerized Emily

Dickinson, Lowell was overwhelmed by poems she understood had come in part from Dickinson's seclusion, her "carelessness in the matter of whether she exists for her readers . . . " A final crucial influence would come in 1915 when she read Pound's *Cathay* and discovered classical Chinese poetry.

As she corrected proofs of *A Dome of Many-Coloured Glass*, Lowell's work was already changing, but what contribution would life itself make? In a diary at fifteen, she had written, "I feel very much in need of a very intimate friend, a friend whom I should love better than any other girl in the world, & who would feel so towards me. To whom I could tell all that is in my heart & who would do so to me. We should love to be alone together, both of us." Lowell had lived and written obedient to patterns of genteel formality, but she had ferocious hunger for the unpredictable experiences of intimacy and requited passion. A crush on the operetta diva Lisa Abarbanell went no further than trivial friendship, and falling in love with Carl Engel, an urbane French-trained composer, led only to the exchange of intellectual and aesthetic passions (it was to Engel that Lowell articulated the despair she felt at reaching her late thirties, having "managed so badly as to carve out for myself a life made of ashes and fog").

On March 12, 1912, six months before *A Dome of Many-Coloured Glass* was published, at a weekly lunch with women friends, Lowell met Ada Dwyer Russell, a veteran American character actress appearing in Boston in Paul Armstrong's *The Deep Purple*. A divorcée from Salt Lake City where her father had run Dwyer's, for decades the only literary bookstore in the Far West, Ada was a voracious reader. As an actress, she had become famous in Eleanor Robson's company, but once Robson abandoned the stage to marry August Belmont, Ada was left to the-atrical piecework. Eleven years older than Amy, she was a brunette with extraordinary dark eyes, a calming aura, and great intelligence. She was charmed to talk about poetry.

That Sunday, after supper at Sevenels, Amy read Ada the entire text of *A Dome of Many-Coloured Glass*, and two years later Ada retired from the stage to live at Sevenels. When *Sword Blades and Poppy Seed* made Amy famous in 1914, its most powerful poems were love lyrics to Mrs. Russell. Her passion restrained by Imagist discipline, Amy wrote lines that bristled with new intensity—from "The Taxi":

> I call out for you against the jutted stars
> And shout into the ridges of the wind.
> Streets coming fast,
> One after the other,
> Wedge you away from me,
> And the lamps of the city prick my eyes
> So that I can no longer see your face.
> Why should I leave you,
> To wound myself upon the sharp edges of the night?

Ada took on the household of Sevenels, releasing Amy further to her poetry. Beginning at midnight, the private Amy Lowell settled into her enormous library to write through the night, finishing at dawn. It was Ada who made this night work possible, directing that a cold supper be set out on the library table, that last night's drafts be cleanly typed by the staff of secretaries, that no one disturb the poet at work. To Amy's friends and correspondents, Ada was affectionately "Mrs. Russell"—to Amy, she was "Peter," becoming so integral to the life of her writing that Amy imagined for the Sevenels driveway a sign saying "Lowell and Russell, Makers of Fine Poems."

Boston was a city whose name for decades had been given to woman-woman relationships, but the sexuality of Boston marriages was never spoken of, so when Lowell identified as female the addressee of a group of love lyrics in her fourth collection, it was an act of courage. The poems in "Planes of Personality: Two Speak Together" from *Pictures of the Floating World* share the erotic force of earlier poems to Ada, but they are notable for their infusion of domestic detail with a lover's ardor. Here, from "Madonna of the Evening Flowers":

> You tell me that the peonies need spraying,
> That the columbines have overrun all bounds,
> That the pyrus japonica should be cut back and
>   rounded.
> You tell me these things.
> But I look at you, heart of silver,
> White heart-flame or polished silver,
> Burning beneath the blue steeples of the larkspur,
> And I long to kneel instantly at your feet, . . .

The public Amy Lowell knelt at no one's feet. After waking in midafternoon, she worked assiduously to create a cultural context for her work and that of her fellow "new" poets, pursuing her own career and planning her performances with coaching from Ada Russell. She edited anthologies, delivered lectures that became books of essays, argued her progressive ideas about poetry in forums like the Poetry Society of America, defended friends like D. H. Lawrence against uncomprehending critics, wrote countless reviews and occasional pieces for journals like *The New Republic* and *The Century*, becoming central to literary politics and poetic discourse of her time. "The life of a poet is by no means the dreamy aesthetic one most people imagine it to be," she wrote. "A mixture of day-laborer, traveling salesman, and an itinerant actress is what it amounts to."

Lowell rarely flagged—it's typical that she turned an interest in Chinese poetry into a book of translations on which she collaborated with Florence Ayscough, a Chinese-speaking school friend who lived in Shanghai; typical as well that she addressed her critical adversaries in verse. The anonymous publication of the book-length *A Critical Fable* (inspired by James Russell Lowell's *A Fable for Critics*) testifies to her gift for publicity—months of public speculation as to its authorship followed its appearance at the height of her fame in 1922.

This volume is the most extensive collection of Amy Lowell's poems since the Untermeyer edition in 1955 and includes examples of every kind of poem she wrote, poems from eight of her collections, and from *Fir-Flower Tablets*, the Chinese translations. To avoid excerpting, selections from *Can Grande's Castle* and *A Critical Fable* have been omitted, but one can find a taste of her critical brio in "Astigmatism," a verse rendering of her ongoing argument with Ezra Pound, and in "The Sisters," the meditation on Sappho, Mrs. Browning, and Dickinson as female poets. "I wonder what it is that makes us do it," she wrote,

> Singles us out to scribble down, man-wise,
> The fragments of ourselves. Why are we
> Already mother-creatures, double-bearing,
> With matrices in body and in brain?

For much of their life together, Amy and Ada summered in Dublin, New Hampshire. One afternoon in 1916, the horse pulling their wagon, suddenly frightened by an oncoming storm, veered up a mountain, knocking their conveyance into a ditch. Both women got out, and while Ada held the horse's head, Amy, who had been driving, lifted the wagon back onto the road, tearing her umbilical muscles. She felt nothing more than a slight twinge, but the injury was serious and eight years of painful surgeries failed to mend the damage.

Though the pain became debilitating, Lowell slowed down only toward the very end of her life, when, in the Sky Parlour, her lifelong bedroom on the third floor of Sevenels, she received visitors and held meetings, presiding from the vast expanse of her enormous bed. Her biography of Keats appeared in February of 1925, and she had finished correcting proofs of *What's O'Clock* when, on the morning of May 12, standing at her mirror as Ada and a nurse helped her adjust her bandages, she saw the right side of her face drop and understood she was dying. "Pete," she said in a low voice, "a stroke." An hour and a half later, minutes before the doctor's arrival, she died in her bed, Ada at her side. She was fifty-one. On May 15, her ashes were placed in the family plot at Mount Auburn Cemetery in Cambridge, and the next year *What's O'Clock* received the Pulitzer Prize. Years before, in a poem written in the dark of night, Amy had imagined leaving life, Sevenels, and her beloved Ada:

> The old house will guard you
> As I have done.
> Its walls and rooms will hold you,
> And I shall whisper my thoughts and fancies
> As always,
> From the pages of my books.

Honor Moore
2004

Apples of Hesperides

Glinting golden through the trees,
   Apples of Hesperides!
Through the moon-pierced warp of night
Shoot pale shafts of yellow light,
Swaying to the kissing breeze
Swings the treasure, golden-gleaming,
         Apples of Hesperides!

Far and lofty yet they glimmer,
   Apples of Hesperides!
Blinded by their radiant shimmer,
Pushing forward just for these;
Dew-besprinkled, bramble-marred,
Poor duped mortal, travel-scarred,
Always thinking soon to seize
And possess the golden-glistening
         Apples of Hesperides!

Orbed, and glittering, and pendent,
   Apples of Hesperides!
Not one missing, still transcendent,
Clustering like a swarm of bees.
Yielding to no man's desire,
Glowing with a saffron fire,
Splendid, unassailed, the golden
         Apples of Hesperides!

ΔΙΨΑ

Look, Dear, how bright the moonlight is to-night!
See where it casts the shadow of that tree
Far out upon the grass. And every gust
Of light night wind comes laden with the scent
Of opening flowers which never bloom by day:
Night-scented stocks, and four-o'clocks, and that
Pale yellow disk, upreared on its tall stalk,
The evening primrose, comrade of the stars.
It seems as though the garden which you love
Were like a swinging censer, its incense
Floating before us as a reverent act
To sanctify and bless our night of love.
Tell me once more you love me, that 't is you
Yes, really you, I touch, so, with my hand;
And tell me it is by your own free will
That you are here, and that you like to be
Just here, with me, under this sailing pine.
I need to hear it often for my heart
Doubts naturally, and finds it hard to trust.
Ah, Dearest, you are good to love me so,
And yet I would not have it goodness, rather
Excess of selfishness in you to need
Me through and through, as flowers need the sun.
I wonder can it really be that you
And I are here alone, and that the night
Is full of hours, and all the world asleep,
And none can call to you to come away;
For you have given all yourself to me
Making me gentle by your willingness.

Has your life too been waiting for this time,
Not only mine the sharpness of this joy?
Dear Heart, I love you, worship you as though
I were a priest before a holy shrine.
I'm glad that you are beautiful, although
Were you not lovely still I needs must love;
But you are all things, it must have been so
For otherwise it were not you. Come, close;
When you are in the circle of my arm
Faith grows a mountain and I take my stand
Upon its utmost top. Yes, yes, once more
Kiss me, and let me feel you very near
Wanting me wholly, even as I want you.
Have years behind been dark? Will those to come
Bring unguessed sorrows into our two lives?
What does it matter, we have had to-night!
To-night will make us strong, for we believe
Each in the other, this is a sacrament.
Beloved, is it true?

On Carpaccio's Picture
The Dream of St. Ursula

Swept, clean, and still, across the polished floor
    From some unshuttered casement, hid from sight,
    The level sunshine slants, its greater light
Quenching the little lamp which pallid, poor,
Flickering, unreplenished, at the door
    Has striven against darkness the long night.

Dawn fills the room, and penetrating, bright,
The silent sunbeams through the window pour.
   And she lies sleeping, ignorant of Fate,
   Enmeshed in listless dreams, her soul not yet
Ripened to bear the purport of this day.
   The morning breeze scarce stirs the coverlet,
   A shadow falls across the sunlight; wait!
A lark is singing as he flies away.

The Matrix

Goaded and harassed in the factory
   That tears our life up into bits of days
   Ticked off upon a clock which never stays,
Shredding our portion of Eternity,
We break away at last, and steal the key
   Which hides a world empty of hours; ways
   Of space unroll, and Heaven overlays
The leafy, sun-lit earth of Fantasy.
   Beyond the ilex shadow glares the sun,
   Scorching against the blue flame of the sky.
Brown lily-pads lie heavy and supine
   Within a granite basin, under one
   The bronze-gold glimmer of a carp; and I
Reach out my hand and pluck a nectarine.

A Fixed Idea

What torture lurks within a single thought
When grown too constant, and however kind,
However welcome still, the weary mind
Aches with its presence. Dull remembrance taught
Remembers on unceasingly; unsought
The old delight is with us but to find
That all recurring joy is pain refined,
Become a habit, and we struggle, caught.
You lie upon my heart as on a nest,
Folded in peace, for you can never know
How crushed I am with having you at rest
Heavy upon my life. I love you so
You bind my freedom from its rightful quest.
In mercy lift your drooping wings and go.

Crépuscule du matin

All night I wrestled with a memory
    Which knocked insurgent at the gates of thought.
    The crumbled wreck of years behind has wrought
Its disillusion; now I only cry
For peace, for power to forget the lie
    Which hope too long has whispered. So I sought
    The sleep which would not come, and night was
        fraught
With old emotions weeping silently.

I heard your voice again, and knew the things
    Which you had promised proved an empty vaunt.
I felt your clinging hands while night's broad wings
Cherished our love in darkness. From the lawn
    A sudden, quivering birdnote, like a taunt.
My arms held nothing but the empty dawn.

The Starling

"'I can't get out,' said the starling."
        STERNE'S *Sentimental Journey.*

Forever the impenetrable wall
    Of self confines my poor rebellious soul,
    I never see the towering white clouds roll
Before a sturdy wind, save through the small
Barred window of my jail. I live a thrall
    With all my outer life a clipped, square hole,
    Rectangular; a fraction of a scroll
Unwound and winding like a worsted ball.
    My thoughts are grown uneager and depressed
    Through being always mine, my fancy's wings
Are moulted and the feathers blown away.
    I weary for desires never guessed,
    For alien passions, strange imaginings,
To be some other person for a day.

The Painted Ceiling

My Grandpapa lives in a wonderful house
　　With a great many windows and doors,
There are stairs that go up, and stairs that go down,
　　And such beautiful, slippery floors.

But of all of the rooms, even mother's and mine,
　　And the bookroom, and parlour and all,
I like the green dining-room so much the best
　　Because of its ceiling and wall.

Right over your head is a funny round hole
　　With apples and pears falling through;
There's a big bunch of grapes all purply and sweet,
　　And melons and pineapples too.

They tumble and tumble, but never come down
　　Though I've stood underneath a long while
With my mouth open wide, for I always have hoped
　　Just a cherry would drop from the pile.

No matter how early I run there to look
　　It has always begun to fall through;
And one night when at bedtime I crept in to see,
　　It was falling by candle-light too.

I am sure they are magical fruits, and each one
　　Makes you hear things, or see things, or go
Forever invisible; but it's no use,
　　And of course I shall just never know.

For the ladder's too heavy to lift, and the chairs
    Are not nearly so tall as I need.
I've given up hope, and I feel I shall die
    Without having accomplished the deed.

It's a little bit sad, when you seem very near
    To adventures and things of that sort,
Which nearly begin, and then don't; and you know
    It is only because you are short.

Climbing

High up in the apple tree climbing I go,
With the sky above me, the earth below.
Each branch is the step of a wonderful stair
Which leads to the town I see shining up there.

Climbing, climbing, higher and higher,
The branches blow and I see a spire,
The gleam of a turret, the glint of a dome,
All sparkling and bright, like white sea foam.

On and on, from bough to bough,
The leaves are thick, but I push my way through;
Before, I have always had to stop,
But to-day I am sure I shall reach the top.

Today to the end of the marvelous stair,
Where those glittering pinnacles flash in the air!
Climbing, climbing, higher I go,
With the sky close above me, the earth far below.

The Captured Goddess

Over the housetops,
Above the rotating chimney-pots,
I have seen a shiver of amethyst,
And blue and cinnamon have flickered
A moment,
At the far end of a dusty street.

Through sheeted rain
Has come a lustre of crimson,
And I have watched moonbeams
Hushed by a film of palest green.

It was her wings,
Goddess!
Who stepped over the clouds,
And laid her rainbow feathers
Aslant on the currents of the air.

I followed her for long,
With gazing eyes and stumbling feet.
I cared not where she led me,
My eyes were full of colours:
Saffrons, rubies, the yellows of beryls,

And the indigo-blue of quartz;
Flights of rose, layers of chrysoprase,
Points of orange, spirals of vermilion,
The spotted gold of tiger-lily petals,
The loud pink of bursting hydrangeas.
I followed,
And watched for the flashing of her wings.

In the city I found her,
The narrow-streeted city.
In the market-place I came upon her,
Bound and trembling.
Her fluted wings were fastened to her sides with cords,
She was naked and cold,
For that day the wind blew
Without sunshine.

Men chaffered for her,
They bargained in silver and gold,
In copper, in wheat,
And called their bids across the market-place.

The Goddess wept.

Hiding my face I fled,
And the grey wind hissed behind me,
Along the narrow streets.

A London Thoroughfare. 2 A.M.

They have watered the street,
It shines in the glare of lamps,
Cold, white lamps,
And lies
Like a slow-moving river,
Barred with silver and black.
Cabs go down it,
One,
And then another.
Between them I hear the shuffling of feet.
Tramps doze on the window-ledges,
Night-walkers pass along the sidewalks.
The city is squalid and sinister,
With the silver-barred street in the midst,
Slow-moving,
A river leading nowhere.

Opposite my window,
The moon cuts,
Clear and round,
Through the plum-coloured night.
She cannot light the city;
It is too bright.
It has white lamps,
And glitters coldly.

I stand in the window and watch the moon.
She is thin and lustreless,
But I love her.
I know the moon,
And this is an alien city.

Astigmatism

To Ezra Pound
with much friendship and admiration and some differences of opinion

The Poet took his walking-stick
Of fine and polished ebony.
Set in the close-grained wood
Were quaint devices;
Patterns in ambers,
And in the clouded green of jades.
The top was of smooth, yellow ivory,
And a tassel of tarnished gold
Hung by a faded cord from a hole
Pierced in the hard wood,
Circled with silver.
For years the Poet had wrought upon this cane.
His wealth had gone to enrich it,
His experiences to pattern it,
His labour to fashion and burnish it.
To him it was perfect,
A work of art and a weapon,
A delight and a defence.
The Poet took his walking-stick
And walked abroad.

Peace be with you, Brother.

The Poet came to a meadow.
Sifted through the grass were daisies,
Open-mouthed, wondering, they gazed at the sun.

The Poet struck them with his cane.
The little heads flew off, and they lay
Dying, open-mouthed and wondering,
On the hard ground.
"They are useless. They are not roses," said the Poet.

Peace be with you, Brother. Go your ways.

The Poet came to a stream.
Purple and blue flags waded in the water;
In among them hopped the speckled frogs;
The wind slid through them, rustling.
The Poet lifted his cane,
And the iris heads fell into the water.
They floated away, torn and drowning.
"Wretched flowers," said the Poet,
"They are not roses."

Peace be with you, Brother. It is your affair.

The Poet came to a garden.
Dahlias ripened against a wall,
Gillyflowers stood up bravely for all their short stature,
And a trumpet-vine covered an arbour
With the red and gold of its blossoms.
Red and gold like the brass notes of trumpets.
The Poet knocked off the stiff heads of the dahlias,
And his cane lopped the gillyflowers at the ground.
Then he severed the trumpet-blossoms from their stems.

Red and gold they lay scattered,
Red and gold, as on a battle field;
Red and gold, prone and dying.
"They were not roses," said the Poet.

Peace be with you, Brother.
But behind you is destruction, and waste places.

The Poet came home at evening,
And in the candle-light
He wiped and polished his cane.
The orange candle flame leaped in the yellow ambers,
And made the jades undulate like green pools.
It played along the bright ebony,
And glowed in the top of cream-coloured ivory.
But these things were dead,
Only the candle-light made them seem to move.
"It is a pity there were no roses," said the Poet.

Peace be with you, Brother. You have chosen your part.

Apology

Be not angry with me that I bear
　　Your colours everywhere,
　　All through each crowded street,
　　　　And meet
　　The wonder-light in every eye,
　　　　As I go by.

Each plodding wayfarer looks up to gaze,
　　Blinded by rainbow haze,
　　The stuff of happiness,
　　　　No less,
　　Which wraps me in its glad-hued folds
　　　　Of peacock golds.

Before my feet the dusty, rough-paved way
　　Flushes beneath its gray.
　　My steps fall ringed with light,
　　　　So bright,
　　It seems a myriad suns are strown
　　　　About the town.

Around me is the sound of steepled bells,
　　And rich perfuméd smells
　　Hang like a wind-forgotten cloud,
　　　　And shroud
　　Me from close contact with the world.
　　　　I dwell impearled.

You blazon me with jewelled insignia.
    A flaming nebula
    Rims in my life. And yet
       You set
    The word upon me, unconfessed
       To go unguessed.

A Petition

I pray to be the tool which to your hand
    Long use has shaped and moulded till it be
    Apt for your need, and, unconsideringly,
You take it for its service. I demand
To be forgotten in the woven strand
    Which grows the multi-coloured tapestry
    Of your bright life, and through its tissues lie
A hidden, strong, sustaining, grey-toned band.
    I wish to dwell around your daylight dreams,
The railing to the stairway of the clouds,
    To guard your steps securely up, where streams
A faëry moonshine washing pale the crowds
    Of pointed stars. Remember not whereby
    You mount, protected, to the far-flung sky.

Absence

My cup is empty to-night,
Cold and dry are its sides,
Chilled by the wind from the open window.
Empty and void, it sparkles white in the moonlight.
The room is filled with the strange scent
Of wistaria blossoms.
They sway in the moon's radiance
And tap against the wall.
But the cup of my heart is still,
And cold, and empty.

When you come, it brims
Red and trembling with blood,
Heart's blood for your drinking;
To fill your mouth with love
And the bitter-sweet taste of a soul.

A Gift

See! I give myself to you, Beloved!
My words are little jars
For you to take and put upon a shelf.
Their shapes are quaint and beautiful,
And they have many pleasant colours and lustres
To recommend them.
Also the scent from them fills the room
With sweetness of flowers and crushed grasses.

When I shall have given you the last one,
You will have the whole of me,
But I shall be dead.

The Bungler

You glow in my heart
Like the flames of uncounted candles.
But when I go to warm my hands,
My clumsiness overturns the light,
And then I stumble
Against the tables and chairs.

Anticipation

I have been temperate always,
But I am like to be very drunk
With your coming.
There have been times
I feared to walk down the street
Lest I should reel with the wine of you,
And jerk against my neighbours
As they go by.
I am parched now, and my tongue is horrible in my mouth,
But my brain is noisy
With the clash and gurgle of filling wine-cups.

The Taxi

When I go away from you
The world beats dead
Like a slackened drum.
I call out for you against the jutted stars
And shout into the ridges of the wind.
Streets coming fast,
One after the other,
Wedge you away from me,
And the lamps of the city prick my eyes
So that I can no longer see your face.
Why should I leave you,
To wound myself upon the sharp edges of the night?

The Giver of Stars

Hold your soul open for my welcoming.
Let the quiet of your spirit bathe me
With its clear and rippled coolness,
That, loose-limbed and weary, I find rest,
Outstretched upon your peace, as on a bed of ivory.

Let the flickering flame of your soul play all about me,
That into my limbs may come the keenness of fire,
The life and joy of tongues of flame,
And, going out from you, tightly strung and in tune,
I may rouse the blear-eyed world,
And pour into it the beauty which you have begotten.

The Pike

In the brown water,
Thick and silver-sheened in the sunshine,
Liquid and cool in the shade of the reeds,
A pike dozed.
Lost among the shadows of stems
He lay unnoticed.
Suddenly he flicked his tail,
And a green-and-copper brightness
Ran under the water.

Out from under the reeds
Came the olive-green light,
And orange flashed up
Through the sun-thickened water.
So the fish passed across the pool,
Green and copper,
A darkness and a gleam,
And the blurred reflections of the willows on the
    opposite bank
Received it.

The Blue Scarf

Pale, with the blue of high zeniths, shimmered over
    with silver, brocaded
In smooth, running patterns, a soft stuff, with dark
    knotted fringes, it lies there,

Warm from a woman's soft shoulders, and my fingers
    close on it, caressing.
Where is she, the woman who wore it? The scent of her
    lingers and drugs me!
A languor, fire-shotted, runs through me, and I crush
    the scarf down on my face,
And gulp in the warmth and the blueness, and my eyes
    swim in cool-tinted heavens.
Around me are columns of marble, and a diapered, sun-
    flickered pavement.
Rose-leaves blow and patter against it. Below the stone
    steps a lute tinkles.

A jar of green jade throws its shadow half over the floor.
    A big-bellied
Frog hops through the sunlight and plops in the gold-
    bubbled water of a basin,
Sunk in the black and white marble. The west wind has
    lifted a scarf
On the seat close beside me, the blue of it is a violent
    outrage of colour.
She draws it more closely about her, and it ripples
    beneath her slight stirring.
Her kisses are sharp buds of fire; and I burn back against
    her, a jewel
Hard and white; a stalked, flaming flower; till I break to
    a handful of cinders,
And open my eyes to the scarf, shining blue in the
    afternoon sunshine.

How loud clocks can tick when a room is empty, and
    one is alone!

Aubade

As I would free the white almond from the green husk
So would I strip your trappings off,
Beloved.
And fingering the smooth and polished kernel
I should see that in my hands glittered a gem beyond
counting.

Patterns

I walk down the garden paths,
And all the daffodils
Are blowing, and the bright blue squills.
I walk down the patterned garden-paths
In my stiff, brocaded gown.
With my powdered hair and jewelled fan,
I too am a rare
Pattern. As I wander down
The garden paths.

My dress is richly figured,
And the train
Makes a pink and silver stain
On the gravel, and the thrift
Of the borders.
Just a plate of current fashion,
Tripping by in high-heeled, ribboned shoes.
Not a softness anywhere about me,
Only whalebone and brocade.
And I sink on a seat in the shade
Of a lime tree. For my passion
Wars against the stiff brocade.
The daffodils and squills
Flutter in the breeze
As they please.

And I weep;
For the lime-tree is in blossom
And one small flower has dropped upon my bosom.

And the plashing of waterdrops
In the marble fountain
Comes down the garden-paths.
The dripping never stops.
Underneath my stiffened gown
Is the softness of a woman bathing in a marble basin,
A basin in the midst of hedges grown
So thick, she cannot see her lover hiding,
But she guesses he is near,
And the sliding of the water
Seems the stroking of a dear
Hand upon her.
What is Summer in a fine brocaded gown!
I should like to see it lying in a heap upon the ground.
All the pink and silver crumpled up on the ground.

I would be the pink and silver as I ran along the paths,
And he would stumble after,
Bewildered by my laughter.
I should see the sun flashing from his sword-hilt and the
        buckles on his shoes.
I would choose
To lead him in a maze along the patterned paths,
A bright and laughing maze for my heavy-booted lover.
Till he caught me in the shade,
And the buttons of his waistcoat bruised my body as he
        clasped me,

Aching, melting, unafraid.
With the shadows of the leaves and the sundrops,
And the plopping of the waterdrops,
All about us in the open afternoon—
I am very like to swoon
With the weight of this brocade,
For the sun sifts through the shade.

Underneath the fallen blossom
In my bosom,
Is a letter I have hid.
It was brought to me this morning by a rider from the
    Duke.
"Madam, we regret to inform you that Lord Hartwell
Died in action Thursday se'nnight."
As I read it in the white, morning sunlight,
The letters squirmed like snakes.
"Any answer, Madam," said my footman.
"No," I told him.
"See that the messenger takes some refreshment.
No, no answer."
And I walked into the garden,
Up and down the patterned paths,
In my stiff, correct brocade.
The blue and yellow flowers stood up proudly in the sun,
Each one.
I stood upright too,
Held rigid to the pattern
By the stiffness of my gown.
Up and down I walked,
Up and down.

In a month he would have been my husband.
In a month, here, underneath this lime,
We would have broke the pattern;
He for me, and I for him,
He as Colonel, I as Lady,
On this shady seat.
He had a whim
That sunlight carried blessing.
And I answered, "It shall be as you have said."
Now he is dead.

In Summer and in Winter I shall walk
Up and down
The patterned garden-paths
In my stiff, brocaded gown.
The squills and daffodils
Will give place to pillared roses, and to asters, and to snow.
I shall go
Up and down,
In my gown.
Gorgeously arrayed,
Boned and stayed.
And the softness of my body will be guarded from
        embrace
By each button, hook, and lace.
For the man who should loose me is dead,
Fighting with the Duke in Flanders,
In a pattern called a war.
Christ! What are patterns for?

Spring Day

Bath

The day is fresh-washed and fair, and there is a smell of tulips and narcissus in the air.

The sunshine pours in at the bath-room window and bores through the water in the bath-tub in lathes and planes of greenish-white. It cleaves the water into flaws like a jewel, and cracks it to bright light.

Little spots of sunshine lie on the surface of the water and dance, dance, and their reflections wobble deliciously over the ceiling; a stir of my finger sets them whirring, reeling. I move a foot, and the planes of light in the water jar. I lie back and laugh, and let the green-white water, the sun-flawed beryl water, flow over me. The day is almost too bright to bear, the green water covers me from the too bright day. I will lie here awhile and play with the water and the sun spots.

The sky is blue and high. A crow flaps by the window, and there is a whiff of tulips and narcissus in the air.

Breakfast Table

In the fresh-washed sunlight, the breakfast table is decked and white. It offers itself in flat surrender, tendering tastes, and smells, and colours, and metals, and grains, and the white cloth falls over its side, draped and wide. Wheels of white glitter in the silver coffee-pot, hot and spinning like catherine-wheels, they whirl, and twirl —and my eyes begin to smart, the little white, dazzling wheels prick them like darts. Placid and peaceful, the rolls of bread spread themselves in the sun to bask. A stack of butter-pats, pyramidal, shout orange through the white, scream, flutter, call: "Yellow! Yellow! Yellow!" Coffee steam rises in a stream, clouds the silver tea-service with mist, and twists up into the sunlight, re-volved, involuted, suspiring higher and higher, fluting in a thin spiral up the high blue sky. A crow flies by and croaks at the coffee steam. The day is new and fair with good smells in the air.

Walk

Over the street the white clouds meet, and sheer away without touching.

On the sidewalks, boys are playing marbles. Glass marbles, with amber and blue hearts, roll together and part with a sweet clashing noise. The boys strike them with black and red striped agates. The glass marbles spit crimson when they are hit, and slip into the gutters un-der rushing brown water. I smell tulips and narcissus in the air, but there are no flowers anywhere, only white dust whipping up the street, and a girl with a gay Spring hat and blowing skirts. The dust and the wind flirt at her ankles and her neat, high-heeled patent leather shoes. Tap, tap, the little heels pat the pavement, and the wind rustles among the flowers on her hat.

A water-cart crawls slowly on the other side of the way. It is green and gay with new paint, and rumbles con-tentedly, sprinkling clear water over the white dust. Clear zigzagging water, which smells of tulips and narcissus.

The thickening branches make a pink *grisaille* against the blue sky.

Whoop! The clouds go dashing at each other and sheer away just in time. Whoop! And a man's hat careers down the street in front of the white dust, leaps into the branches of a tree, veers away and trundles ahead of the wind, jarring the sunlight into spokes of rose-colour and green.

A motor-car cuts a swathe through the bright air, sharp-beaked, irresistible, shouting to the wind to make way. A glare of dust and sunshine tosses together behind it, and settles down. The sky is quiet and high, and the morning is fair with fresh-washed air.

Midday and Afternoon

Swirl of crowded streets. Shock and recoil of traffic. The stock-still brick façade of an old church, against which the waves of people lurch and withdraw. Flare of sunshine down side-streets. Eddies of light in the windows of chemists' shops, with their blue, gold, purple jars, darting colours far into the crowd. Loud bangs and tremors, murmurings out of high windows, whirring of machine belts, blurring of horses and motors. A quick spin and shudder of brakes on an electric car, and the jar of a church-bell knocking against the metal blue of the sky. I am a piece of the town, a bit of blown dust, thrust along with the crowd. Proud to feel the pavement under me, reeling with feet. Feet tripping, skipping, lagging, dragging, plodding doggedly, or springing up and advancing on firm elastic insteps. A boy is selling papers,

I smell them clean and new from the press. They are fresh like the air, and pungent as tulips and narcissus.

The blue sky pales to lemon, and great tongues of gold blind the shop-windows, putting out their contents in a flood of flame.

Night and Sleep

The day takes her ease in slippered yellow. Electric signs gleam out along the shop fronts, following each other. They grow, and grow, and blow into patterns of fire-flowers as the sky fades. Trades scream in spots of light at the unruffled night. Twinkle, jab, snap, that means a new play; and over the way: plop, drop, quiver, is the sidelong sliver of a watchmaker's sign with its length on another street. A gigantic mug of beer effervesces to the atmosphere over a tall building, but the sky is high and has her own stars, why should she heed ours?

I leave the city with speed. Wheels whirl to take me back to my trees and my quietness. The breeze which blows with me is fresh-washed and clean, it has come but recently from the high sky. There are no flowers in bloom yet, but the earth of my garden smells of tulips and narcissus.

My room is tranquil and friendly. Out of the window I can see the distant city, a band of twinkling gems, little flower-heads with no stems. I cannot see the beer-glass, nor the letters of the restaurants and shops I passed, now the signs blur and all together make the city, glowing on a night of fine weather, like a garden stirring and blowing for the Spring.

The night is fresh-washed and fair and there is a whiff of flowers in the air.

Wrap me close, sheets of lavender. Pour your blue and purple dreams into my ears. The breeze whispers at the shutters and mutters queer tales of old days, and cobbled streets, and youths leaping their horses down marble stairways. Pale blue lavender, you are the colour of the sky when it is fresh-washed and fair . . . I smell the stars . . . they are like tulips and narcissus . . . I smell them in the air.

The Dinner-Party

Fish

"So . . ." they said,
With their wine-glasses delicately poised,
Mocking at the thing they cannot understand.
"So . . ." they said again,
Amused and insolent.
The silver on the table glittered,
And the red wine in the glasses
Seemed the blood I had wasted
In a foolish cause.

Game

The gentleman with the grey-and-black whiskers
Sneered languidly over his quail.

Then my heart flew up and laboured,
And I burst from my own holding
And hurled myself forward.
With straight blows I beat upon him,
Furiously, with red-hot anger, I thrust against him.
But my weapon slithered over his polished surface,
And I recoiled upon myself,
Panting.

Drawing-Room

In a dress all softness and half-tones,
Indolent and half-reclined,
She lay upon a couch,
With the firelight reflected in her jewels.
But her eyes had no reflection,
They swam in a grey smoke,
The smoke of smouldering ashes,
The smoke of her cindered heart.

Coffee

They sat in a circle with their coffee-cups.
One dropped in a lump of sugar,
One stirred with a spoon.
I saw them as a circle of ghosts
Sipping blackness out of beautiful china,
And mildly protesting against my coarseness
In being alive.

Talk

They took dead men's souls
And pinned them on their breasts for ornament;
Their cuff-links and tiaras
Were gems dug from a grave;
They were ghouls battening on exhumed thoughts;
And I took a green liqueur from a servant
So that he might come near me
And give me the comfort of a living thing.

Eleven O'Clock

The front door was hard and heavy,
It shut behind me on the house of ghosts.
I flattened my feet on the pavement
To feel it solid under me;
I ran my hand along the railings
And shook them,
And pressed their pointed bars
Into my palms.
The hurt of it reassured me,
And I did it again and again
Until they were bruised.
When I woke in the night
I laughed to find them aching,
For only living flesh can suffer.

Towns in Colour

I   Red Slippers

Red slippers in a shop-window, and outside in the street, flaws of grey, windy sleet!

Behind the polished glass, the slippers hang in long threads of red, festooning from the ceiling like stalactites of blood, flooding the eyes of passers-by with dripping colour, jamming their crimson reflections against the windows of cabs and tram-cars, screaming their claret and salmon into the teeth of the sleet, plopping their little round maroon lights upon the tops of umbrellas.

The row of white, sparkling shop fronts is gashed and bleeding, it bleeds red slippers. They spout under the electric light, fluid and fluctuating, a hot rain—and freeze again to red slippers, myriadly multiplied in the mirror side of the window.

They balance upon arched insteps like springing bridges of crimson lacquer; they swing up over curved heels like whirling tanagers sucked in a wind-pocket; they flatten out, heelless, like July ponds, flared and burnished by red rockets.

Snap, snap, they are cracker-sparks of scarlet in the white, monotonous block of shops.

They plunge the clangour of billions of vermilion trumpets into the crowd outside, and echo in faint rose over the pavement.

People hurry by, for these are only shoes, and in a window, farther down, is a big lotus bud of cardboard whose petals open every few minutes and reveal a wax doll, with staring bead eyes and flaxen hair, lolling awkwardly in its flower chair.

One has often seen shoes, but whoever saw a cardboard lotus bud before?

The flaws of grey, windy sleet beat on the shop-window where there are only red slippers.

II   *Thompson's Lunch Room—Grand Central Station*

Study in Whites

Wax-white—
Floor, ceiling, walls.
Ivory shadows
Over the pavement
Polished to cream surfaces
By constant sweeping.
The big room is coloured like the petals
Of a great magnolia,
And has a patina
Of flower bloom
Which makes it shine dimly
Under the electric lamps.
Chairs are ranged in rows
Like sepia seeds
Waiting fulfilment.
The chalk-white spot of a cook's cap

Moves unglossily against the vaguely bright wall—
Dull chalk-white striking the retina like a blow
Through the wavering uncertainty of steam.
Vitreous-white of glasses with green reflections,
Ice-green carboys, shifting—greener, bluer—with the
jar of moving water.
Jagged green-white bowls of pressed glass
Rearing snow-peaks of chipped sugar
Above the lighthouse-shaped castors
Of grey pepper and grey-white salt.
Grey-white placards: "Oyster Stew, Cornbeef Hash,
Frankfurters":
Marble slabs veined with words in meandering lines.
Dropping on the white counter like horn notes
Through a web of violins,
The flat yellow lights of oranges,
The cube-red splashes of apples,
In high plated *épergnes.*
The electric clock jerks every half-minute:
"Coming!—Past!"
"Three beef-steaks and a chicken-pie,"
Bawled through a slide while the clock jerks heavily.
A man carries a china mug of coffee to a distant chair.
Two rice puddings and a salmon salad
Are pushed over the counter;
The unfulfilled chairs open to receive them.
A spoon falls upon the floor with the impact of metal
striking stone,
And the sound throws across the room
Sharp, invisible zigzags
Of silver.

III   An Opera House

Within the gold square of the proscenium arch,
A curtain of orange velvet hangs in stiff folds,
Its tassels jarring slightly when someone crosses the
      stage behind.
Gold carving edges the balconies,
Rims the boxes,
Runs up and down fluted pillars.
Little knife-stabs of gold
Shine out whenever a box door is opened.
Gold clusters
Flash in soft explosions
On the blue darkness,
Suck back to a point,
And disappear.
Hoops of gold
Circle necks, wrists, fingers,
Pierce ears,
Poise on heads
And fly up above them in coloured sparkles.
Gold!
Gold!
The opera house is a treasure-box of gold.
Gold in a broad smear across the orchestra pit:
Gold of horns, trumpets, tubas;
Gold—spun-gold, twittering-gold, snapping-gold
Of harps.
The conductor raises his baton,
The brass blares out
Crass, crude,

Parvenu, fat, powerful,
Golden.
Rich as the fat, clapping hands in the boxes.
Cymbals, gigantic, coin-shaped,
Crash.
The orange curtain parts
And the prima-donna steps forward.
One note,
A drop: transparent, iridescent,
A gold bubble,
It floats . . . floats . . .
And bursts against the lips of a bank president
In the grand tier.

IV   Afternoon Rain in State Street

Cross-hatchings of rain against grey walls,
Slant lines of black rain
In front of the up and down, wet stone sides of buildings.
Below,
Greasy, shiny, black, horizontal,
The street.
And over it, umbrellas,
Black polished dots
Struck to white
An instant,
Stream in two flat lines
Slipping past each other with the smoothness of oil.
Like a four-sided wedge
The Custom House Tower
Pokes at the low, flat sky,

Pushing it farther and farther up,
Lifting it away from the house-tops,
Lifting it in one piece as though it were a sheet of tin,
With the lever of its apex.
The cross-hatchings of rain cut the Tower obliquely,
Scratching lines of black wire across it,
Mutilating its perpendicular grey surface
With the sharp precision of tools.
The city is rigid with straight lines and angles,
A chequered table of blacks and greys.
Oblong blocks of flatness
Crawl by with low-geared engines,
And pass to short upright squares
Shrinking with distance.
A steamer in the basin blows its whistle,
And the sound shoots across the rain hatchings,
A narrow, level bar of steel.
Hard cubes of lemon
Superimpose themselves upon the fronts of buildings
As the windows light up.
But the lemon cubes are edged with angles
Upon which they cannot impinge.
Up, straight, down, straight—square.
Crumpled grey-white papers
Blow along the side-walks,
Contorted, horrible,
Without curves.
A horse steps in a puddle,
A white, glaring water spurts up
In stiff, outflaring lines,
Like the rattling stems of reeds.

The city is heraldic with angles,
A sombre escutcheon of argent and sable
And countercoloured bends of rain
Hung over a four-square civilization.
When a street lamp comes out,
I gaze at it for full thirty seconds
To rest my brain with the suffusing, round brilliance of
    its globe.

V   An Aquarium

Streaks of green and yellow iridescence,
Silver shiftings,
Rings veering out of rings,
Silver—gold—
Grey-green opaqueness sliding down,
With sharp white bubbles
Shooting and dancing,
Flinging quickly outward.
Nosing the bubbles,
Swallowing them,
Fish.
Blue shadows against silver-saffron water,
The light rippling over them
In steel-bright tremors.
Outspread translucent fins
Flute, fold, and relapse;
The threaded light prints through them on the pebbles
In scarcely tarnished twinklings.
Curving of spotted spines,
Slow up-shifts,

Lazy convolutions:
Then a sudden swift straightening
And darting below:
Oblique grey shadows
Athwart a pale casement.
Roped and curled,
Green man-eating eels
Slumber in undulate rhythms,
With crests laid horizontal on their backs.
Barred fish,
Striped fish,
Uneven disks of fish,
Slip, slide, whirl, turn,
And never touch.
Metallic blue fish,
With fins wide and yellow and swaying
Like Oriental fans,
Hold the sun in their bellies
And glow with light:
Blue brilliance cut by black bars.
An oblong pane of straw-coloured shimmer,
Across it, in a tangent,
A smear of rose, black, silver.
Short twists and upstartings,
Rose-black, in a setting of bubbles:
Sunshine playing between red and black flowers
On a blue and gold lawn.
Shadows and polished surfaces,
Facets of mauve and purple,
A constant modulation of values.
Shaft-shaped,

With green bead eyes;
Thick-nosed,
Heliotrope-coloured;
Swift spots of chrysolite and coral;
In the midst of green, pearl, amethyst irradiations.

Outside,
A willow-tree flickers
With little white jerks,
And long blue waves
Rise steadily beyond the outer islands.

PICTURES OF THE FLOATING WORLD | 1919

Streets

(Adapted from the poet Yakura Sanjin, 1769)

As I wandered through the eight hundred and eight
    streets of the city,
I saw nothing so beautiful
As the Women of the Green Houses,
With their girdles of spun gold,
And their long-sleeved dresses,
Coloured like the graining of wood.
As they walk,
The hems of their outer garments flutter open,
And the blood-red linings glow like sharp-toothed
    maple leaves
In Autumn.

Desolation

Under the plum-blossoms are nightingales;
But the sea is hidden in an egg-white mist,
And they are silent.

The Fisherman's Wife

When I am alone,
The wind in the pine-trees
Is like the shuffling of waves
Upon the wooden sides of a boat.

The Pond

Cold, wet leaves
Floating on moss-coloured water,
And the croaking of frogs—
Cracked bell-notes in the twilight.

Autumn

All day I have watched the purple vine leaves
Fall into the water.
And now in the moonlight they still fall,
But each leaf is fringed with silver.

The Camellia Tree of Matsue

At Matsue,
There was a Camellia Tree of great beauty
Whose blossoms were white as honey wax
Splashed and streaked with the pink of fair coral.
At night,
When the moon rose in the sky,
The Camellia Tree would leave its place
By the gateway,
And wander up and down the garden,
Trailing its roots behind it
Like a train of rustling silk.
The people in the house,
Hearing the scrape of them upon the gravel,
Looked out into the garden
And saw the tree,
With its flowers erect and peering,
Pressed against the shōji.
Many nights the tree walked about the garden,
Until the women and children
Became frightened,
And the Master of the house
Ordered that it be cut down.
But when the gardener brought his axe
And struck at the trunk of the tree,
There spouted forth a stream of dark blood;
And when the stump was torn up,
The hold quivered like an open wound.

Superstition

I have painted a picture of a ghost
Upon my kite,
And hung it on a tree.
Later, when I loose the string
And let it fly,
The people will cower
And hide their heads,
For fear of the God
Swimming in the clouds.

The Return

Coming up from my boat
In haste to lighten your anxiety,
I saw, reflected in the circular metal mirror,
The face and hands of a woman
Arranging her hair.

In Time of War

Across the newly-plastered wall,
The darting of red dragonflies
Is like the shooting
Of blood-tipped arrows.

Time

Looking at myself in my metal mirror,
I saw, faintly outlined,
The figure of a crane
Engraved upon its back.

Passing the Bamboo Fence

What fell upon my open umbrella—
A plum-blossom?

A Burnt Offering

Because there was no wind,
The smoke of your letters hung in the air
For a long time;
And its shape
Was the shape of your face,
My Beloved.

Reflections

When I looked into your eyes,
I saw a garden

With peonies, and tinkling pagodas,
And round-arched bridges
Over still lakes.
A woman sat beside the water
In a rain-blue, silken garment.
She reached through the water
To pluck the crimson peonies
Beneath the surface,
But as she grasped the stems,
They jarred and broke into white-green ripples;
And as she drew out her hand,
The water-drops dripping from it
Stained her rain-blue dress like tears.

A Poet's Wife

Cho Wēn-chün to her husband Ssŭ-ma Hsiang-ju

You have taken our love and turned it into coins of
   silver.
You sell the love poems you wrote for me,
And with the price of them you buy many cups of wine.
I beg that you remain dumb,
That you write no more poems.
For the wine does us both an injury,
And the words of your heart
Have become the common speech of the Emperor's
   concubines.

Spring Longing

The South wind blows open the folds of my dress,
My feet leave wet tracks in the earth of my garden,
The willows along the canal sing
                with new leaves turned upon the wind.

  I walk along the tow-path
  Gazing at the level water.
  Should I see a ribbed edge
  Running upon its clearness,
  I should know that this was caused
  By the prow of the boat
  In which you are to return.

Vernal Equinox

The scent of hyacinths, like a pale mist, lies between me
    and my book;
And the South Wind, washing through the room,
Makes the candles quiver.
My nerves sting at a spatter of rain on the shutter,
And I am uneasy with the thrusting of green shoots
Outside, in the night.

Why are you not here to overpower me with your tense
    and urgent love?

The Letter

Little cramped words scrawling all over the paper
Like draggled fly's legs,
What can you tell of the flaring moon
Through the oak leaves?
Or of my uncurtained window and the bare floor
Spattered with moonlight?
Your silly quirks and twists have nothing in them
Of blossoming hawthorns,
And this paper is dull, crisp, smooth, virgin of loveliness
Beneath my hand.

I am tired, Beloved, of chafing my heart against
The want of you;
Of squeezing it into little inkdrops,
And posting it.
And I scald alone, here, under the fire
Of the great moon.

Mise en Scène

When I think of you, Beloved,
I see a smooth and stately garden
With parterres of gold and crimson tulips
And bursting lilac leaves.
There is a low-lipped basin in the midst,
Where a statue of veined cream marble
Perpetually pours water over her shoulder

From a rounded urn.
When the wind blows,
The water-stream blows before it
And spatters into the basin with a light tinkling,
And your shawl—the colour of red violets—
Flares out behind you in great curves
Like the swirling draperies of a painted Madonna.

Venus Transiens

Tell me,
Was Venus more beautiful
Than you are,
When she topped
The crinkled waves,
Drifting shoreward
On her plaited shell?
Was Botticelli's vision
Fairer than mine;
And were the painted rosebuds
He tossed his lady,
Of better worth
Than the words I blow about you
To cover your too great loveliness
As with a gauze
Of misted silver?
For me,
You stand poised
In the blue and buoyant air,

Cinctured by bright winds,
Treading the sunlight.
And the waves which precede you
Ripple and stir
The sands at my feet.

Madonna of the Evening Flowers

All day long I have been working,
Now I am tired.
I call: "Where are you?"
But there is only the oak-tree rustling in the wind.
The house is very quiet,
The sun shines in on your books,
On your scissors and thimble just put down,
But you are not there.
Suddenly I am lonely:
Where are you?
I go about searching.

Then I see you,
Standing under a spire of pale blue larkspur,
With a basket of roses on your arm.
You are cool, like silver,
And you smile.
I think the Canterbury bells are playing little tunes.

You tell me that the peonies need spraying,
That the columbines have overrun all bounds,

That the pyrus japonica should be cut back and
   rounded.
You tell me these things.
But I look at you, heart of silver,
White heart-flame of polished silver,
Burning beneath the blue steeples of the larkspur,
And I long to kneel instantly at your feet,
While all about us peal the loud, sweet *Te Deums* of the
   Canterbury bells.

Bright Sunlight

The wind has blown a corner of your shawl
Into the fountain,
Where it floats and drifts
Among the lily-pads
Like a tissue of sapphires.
But you do not heed it,
Your fingers pick at the lichens
On the stone edge of the basin,
And your eyes follow the tall clouds
As they sail over the ilex-trees.

Wheat-in-the-Ear

You stand between the cedars and the green spruces,
Brilliantly naked
And I think:
    What are you,
    A gem under sunlight?
    A poised spear?
    A jade cup?
You flash in front of the cedars and the tall spruces,
And I see that you are fire—
Sacrificial fire on a jade altar,
Spear-tongue of white, ceremonial fire.
My eyes burn,
My hands are flames seeking you,
But you are as remote from me as a bright pointed
      planet
Set in the distance of an evening sky.

The Weather-Cock Points South

I put your leaves aside,
One by one:
The stiff, broad outer leaves;
The smaller ones,
Pleasant to touch, veined with purple;
The glazed inner leaves.

One by one
I parted you from your leaves,
Until you stood up like a white flower
Swaying slightly in the evening wind.

White flower,
Flower of wax, of jade, of unstreaked agate;
Flower with surfaces of ice,
With shadows faintly crimson.
Where in all the garden is there such a flower?
The stars crowd through the lilac leaves
To look at you.
The low moon brightens you with silver.

The bud is more than the calyx.
There is nothing to equal a white bud,
Of no colour, and of all,
Burnished by moonlight,
Thrust upon by a softly-swinging wind.

The Artist

Why do you subdue yourself in golds and purples?
Why do you dim yourself with folded silks?
Do you not see that I can buy brocades in any draper's
    shop,
And that I am choked in the twilight of all these colours.
How pale you would be, and startling,

How quiet;
But your curves would spring upward
Like a clear jet of flung water,
You would quiver like a shot-up spray of water,
You would waver, and relapse, and tremble.
And I too should tremble,
Watching.

Murex-dyes and tinsel—
And yet I think I could bear your beauty unshaded.

The Garden by Moonlight

A black cat among roses,
Phlox, lilac-misted under a first-quarter moon,
The sweet smells of heliotrope and night-scented stock.
The garden is very still,
It is dazed with moonlight,
Contented with perfume,
Dreaming the opium dreams of its folded poppies.
Firefly lights open and vanish
High as the tip buds of the golden glow
Low as the sweet alyssum flowers at my feet.
Moon-shimmer on leaves and trellises,
Moon-spikes shafting through the snow-ball bush.
Only the little faces of the ladies' delight are alert and
        staring,
Only the cat, padding between the roses,
Shakes a branch and breaks the chequered pattern

As water is broken by the falling of a leaf.
Then you come,
And you are quiet like the garden,
And white like the alyssum flowers,
And beautiful as the silent sparks of the fireflies.
Ah, Beloved, do you see those orange lilies?
They knew my mother,
But who belonging to me will they know
When I am gone.

Interlude

When I have baked white cakes
And grated green almonds to spread upon them;
When I have picked the green crowns from the
      strawberries
And piled them, cone-pointed, in a blue and yellow
      platter;
When I have smoothed the seam of the linen I have
      been working;
What then?
To-morrow it will be the same:
Cakes and strawberries,
And needles in and out of cloth.
If the sun is beautiful on bricks and pewter,
How much more beautiful is the moon,
Slanting down the gauffered branches of a plum-tree;
The moon,
Wavering across a bed of tulips;

The moon,
Still,
Upon your face.
You shine, Beloved,
You and the moon.
But which is the reflection?
The clock is striking eleven.
I think, when we have shut and barred the door,
The night will be dark
Outside.

Bullion

My thoughts
Chink against my ribs
And roll about like silver hail-stones.
I should like to spill them out,
And pour them, all shining,
Over you.
But my heart is shut upon them
And holds them straitly.

Come, You! and open my heart;
That my thoughts torment me no longer,
But glitter in your hair.

A Shower

That sputter of rain, flipping the hedge-rows
And making the highways hiss,
How I love it!
And the touch of you upon my arm
As you press against me that my umbrella
May cover you.

Tinkle of drops on stretched silk.
Wet murmur through green branches.

Summer Rain

All night our room was outer-walled with rain.
Drops fell and flattened on the tin roof,
And rang like little disks of metal.
Ping!—Ping!—and there was not a pin-point of silence
    between them.
The rain rattled and clashed,
And the slats of the shutters danced and glittered.
But to me the darkness was red-gold and crocus-
    coloured
With your brightness,
And the words you whispered to me
Sprang up and flamed—orange torches against the rain.
Torches against the wall of cool, silver rain!

After a Storm

You walk under the ice trees.
They sway, and crackle,
And arch themselves splendidly
To deck your going.
The white sun flips them into colour
Before you.
They are blue,
And mauve,
And emerald.
They are amber,
And jade,
And sardonyx.
They are silver fretted to flame
And startled to stillness,
Bunched, splintered, iridescent.
You walk under the ice trees
And the bright snow creaks as you step upon it.
My dogs leap about you,
And their barking strikes upon the air
Like sharp hammer-strokes on metal.
You walk under the ice trees
But you are more dazzling than the ice flowers,
And the dogs' barking
Is not so loud to me as your quietness.

You walk under the ice trees
At ten o'clock in the morning.

Opal

You are ice and fire,
The touch of you burns my hands like snow.
You are cold and flame.
You are the crimson of amaryllis,
The silver of moon-touched magnolias.
When I am with you,
My heart is a frozen pond
Gleaming with agitated torches.

Wakefulness

Jolt of market-carts;
Steady drip of horses' hoofs on hard pavement;
A black sky lacquered over with blueness,
And the lights of Battersea Bridge
Pricking pale in the dawn.
The beautiful hours are passing
And still you sleep!
Tired heart of my joy,
Incurved upon your dreams,
Will the day come before you have opened to me?

Orange of Midsummer

You came to me in the pale starting of Spring,
And I could not see the world
For the blue mist of wonder before my eyes.
You beckoned me over a rainbow bridge,
And I set foot upon it, trembling.
Through pearl and saffron I followed you,
Through heliotrope and rose,
Iridescence after iridescence,
And to me it was all one
Because of the blue mist that held my eyes.

You came again, and it was red-hearted Summer.
You called to me across a field of poppies and wheat,
With a narrow path slicing through it
Straight to an outer boundary of trees.
And I ran along the path,
Brushing over the yellow wheat beside it,
And came upon you under a maple-tree, plaiting
       poppies for a girdle.
"Are you thirsty?" said you,
And held out a cup.
But the water in the cup was scarlet and crimson
Like the poppies in your hands.
"It looks like blood," I said.
"Like blood," you said,
"Does it?
But drink it, my Beloved."

Shore Grass

The moon is cold over the sand-dunes,
And the clumps of sea-grasses flow and glitter;
The thin chime of my watch tells the quarter after
        midnight;
And still I hear nothing
But the windy beating of the sea.

Autumnal Equinox

Why do you not sleep, Beloved?

It is so cold that the stars stand out of the sky
Like golden nails not driven home.
The fire crackles pleasantly,
And I sit here listening
For your regular breathing from the room above.

What keeps you awake, Beloved?
Is it the same nightmare that keeps me strained with
        listening
So that I cannot read?

Nerves

The lake is steel-coloured and umber,
And a clutter of gaunt clouds blows rapidly across the sky.

I wonder why you chose to be buried
In this little grave-yard by the lake-side.
It is all very well on blue mornings,
Summer mornings,
Autumn mornings polished with sunlight.
But in Winter, in the cold storms,
When there is no wind,
And the snow murmurs as it falls!
The grave-stones glimmer in the twilight
As though they were rubbed with phosphorous.
The direct road is up a hill,
Through woods—
I will take the lake road,
I can drive faster there.
You used to like to drive with me—
Why does death make you this fearful thing?
Flick!—flack!—my horse's feet strike the stones.
There is a house just round the bend.

Autumn

They brought me a quilled, yellow dahlia,
Opulent, flaunting.
Round gold
Flung out of a pale green stalk.
Round, ripe gold
Of maturity,
Meticulously frilled and flaming,
A fire-ball of proclamation:
Fecundity decked in staring yellow
For all the world to see.
They brought a quilled, yellow dahlia,
To me who am barren.
Shall I send it to you,
You who have taken with you
All I once possessed?

Strain

It is late
And the clock is striking thin hours,
But sleep has become a terror to me,
Lest I wake in the night
Bewildered,
And stretching out my arms to comfort myself with you,
Clasp instead the cold body of the darkness.
All night it will hunger over me,
And push and undulate against me,

Breathing into my mouth
And passing long fingers through my drifting hair.
Only the dawn can loose me from it,
And the grey streaks of morning melt it from my side.

Bring my candles,
Though they stab my tired brain
And hurt it.
For I am afraid of the twining of the darkness
And dare not sleep.

Haunted

See! He trails his toes
Through the long streaks of moonlight,
And the nails of his fingers glitter:
They claw and flash among the tree-tops.
His lips suck at my open window,
And his breath creeps about my body
And lies in pools under my knees.
I can see his mouth sway and wobble,
Sticking itself against the window-jambs,
But the moonlight is bright on the floor,
Without a shadow.
Hark! A hare is strangling in the forest,
And the wind tears a shutter from the wall.

Grotesque

Why do the lilies goggle their tongues at me
When I pluck them;
And writhe, and twist,
And strangle themselves against my fingers,
So that I can hardly weave the garland,
For your hair?
Why do they shriek your name
And spit at me
When I would cluster them?
Must I kill them
To make them lie still,
And send you a wreath of lolling corpses
To turn putrid and soft
On your forehead
While you dance?

Maladie de l'Après-Midi

Why does the clanking of a tip-cart
In the road
Make me so sad?
The sound beats the air
With flat blows,
Dull and continued.

Not even the clear sunshine
Through bronze and green oak leaves,
Nor the crimson spindle of a cedar-tree

Hooded with Virginia creeper,
Nor the humming brightness of the air,
Can comfort my melancholy.

The cart goes slowly,
It creeps at a foot-pace,
And the flat blows of sound
Hurt me,
And bring me nearly to weeping.

Nostalgia

"Through pleasures and palaces"—
Through hotels, and Pullman cars, and steamships . . .

Pink and white camellias
          floating in a crystal bowl,
The sharp smell of firewood,
The scrape and rustle of a dog stretching himself
          on a hardwood floor,
And your voice, reading—reading—
          to the slow ticking of an old brass clock . . .

"Tickets, please!"
And I watch the man in front of me
Fumbling in fourteen pockets,
While the conductor balances his ticket-punch
Between his fingers.

A Decade

When you came, you were like red wine and honey,
And the taste of you burnt my mouth with its sweetness.
Now you are like morning bread,
Smooth and pleasant.
I hardly taste you at all for I know your savour,
But I am completely nourished.

Penumbra

As I sit here in the quiet Summer night,
Suddenly, from the distant road, there comes
The grind and rush of an electric car.
And, from still farther off,
An engine puffs sharply,
Followed by the drawn-out shunting scrape of a freight
    train.
These are the sounds that men make
In the long business of living.
They will always make such sounds,
Years after I am dead and cannot hear them.

Sitting here in the Summer night,
I think of my death.
What will it be like for you then?
You will see my chair
With its bright chintz covering
Standing in the afternoon sunshine,

As now.
You will see my narrow table
At which I have written so many hours.
My dogs will push their noses into your hand,
And ask—ask—
Clinging to you with puzzled eyes.

The old house will still be here,
The old house which has known me since the beginning.
The walls which have watched me while I played:
Soldiers, marbles, paper-dolls,
Which have protected me and my books.

The front-door will gaze down among the old trees
Where, as a child, I hunted ghosts and Indians;
It will look out on the wide gravel sweep
Where I rolled my hoop,
And at the rhododendron bushes
Where I caught black-spotted butterflies.

The old house will guard you,
As I have done.
Its walls and rooms will hold you,
And I shall whisper my thoughts and fancies
As always,
From the pages of my books.

You will sit here, some quiet Summer night,
Listening to the puffing trains,
But you will not be lonely,
For these things are a part of me.

And my love will go on speaking to you
Through the chairs, and the tables, and the pictures,
As it does now through my voice,
And the quick, necessary touch of my hand.

The Corner of Night and Morning

Crows are cawing over pine-trees,
They are teaching their young to fly
About the tall pyramids of double cherries.
Rose lustre over black lacquer—
The feathers of the young birds reflect the rose-rising
      sun.
Caw! Caw!
I want to go to sleep,
But perhaps it is better to stand in the window
And watch the crows teaching their young to fly
Over the pines and the pyramidal cherries,
In the rose-gold light
Of five o'clock on a May morning.

Beech, Pine, and Sunlight

The sudden April heat
Stretches itself
Under the smooth, leafless branches
Of the beech-tree,

And lies lightly
Upon the great patches
Of purple and white crocus
With their panting, wide-open cups.

A clear wind
Slips through the naked beech boughs,
And their shadows scarcely stir.
But the pine-trees beyond sigh
When it passes over them
And presses back their needles,
And slides gently down their stems.
It is a languor of pale, south-starting sunlight
Come upon a morning unawaked,
And holding her drowsing.

A Bather

After a Picture by Andreas Zorn

Thick dappled by circles of sunshine and fluttering
        shade,
Your bright, naked body advances, blown over by leaves,
Half-quenched in their various green, just a point of you
        showing,
A knee or a thigh, sudden glimpsed, then at once
        blotted into
The filmy and flickering forest, to start out again
Triumphant in smooth, supple roundness, edged sharp
        as white ivory,

Cool, perfect, with rose rarely tinting your lips and your
      breasts,
Swelling out from the green in the opulent curves of
      ripe fruit,
And hidden, like fruit, by the swift intermittence of
      leaves.
So, clinging to branches and moss, you advance on the
      ledges
Of rock which hang over the stream, with the wood-
      smells about you,
The pungence of strawberry plants, and of gum-oozing
      spruces,
While below runs the water, impatient, impatient—to
      take you,
To splash you, to run down your sides, to sing you of
      deepness,
Of pools brown and golden, with brown-and-gold flags
      on their borders,
Of blue, lingering skies floating solemnly over your
      beauty,
Of undulant waters a-sway in the effort to hold you,
To keep you submerged and quiescent while over you
      glories
The Summer.
                  Oread, Dryad, or Naiad, or just
Woman, clad only in youth and in gallant perfection,
Standing up in a great burst of sunshine, you dazzle my
      eyes
Like a snow-star, a moon, your effulgence burns up in a
      halo,
For you are the chalice which holds all the races of men.

You slip into the pool and the water folds over your
    shoulder,
And over the tree-tops the clouds slowly follow your
    swimming,
And the scent of the woods is sweet on this hot Summer
    morning.

Dog-Days

A ladder sticking up at the open window,
The top of an old ladder;
And all of Summer is there.

Great waves and tufts of wistaria surge across the
    window,
And a thin, belated blossom
Jerks up and down in the sunlight;
Purple translucence against the blue sky.
"Tie back this branch," I say,
But my hands are sticky with leaves,
And my nostrils widen to the smell of crushed green.
The ladder moves uneasily at the open window,
And I call to the man beneath,
"Tie back that branch."

There is a ladder leaning against the window-sill,
And a mutter of thunder in the air.

The Travelling Bear

Grass-blades push up between the cobblestones
And catch the sun on their flat sides
Shooting it back,
Gold and emerald,
Into the eyes of passers-by.

And over the cobblestones,
Square-footed and heavy,
Dances the trained bear.
The cobbles cut his feet,
And he has a ring in his nose
Which hurts him;
But still he dances,
For the keeper pricks him with a sharp stick,
Under his fur.

Now the crowd gapes and chuckles,
And boys and young women shuffle their feet in time to
    the dancing bear.
They see him wobbling
Against a dust of emerald and gold,
And they are greatly delighted.

The legs of the bear shake with fatigue,
And his back aches,
And the shining grass-blades dazzle and confuse him.
But still he dances,
Because of the little, pointed stick.

The Broken Fountain

Oblong, its jutted ends rounding into circles,
The old sunken basin lies with its flat, marble lip
An inch below the terrace tiles.
Over the stagnant water
Slide reflections:
The blue-green of coned yews;
The purple and red of trailing fuchsias
Dripping out of marble urns;
Bright squares of sky
Ribbed by the wake of a swimming beetle.
Through the blue-bronze water
Wavers the pale uncertainty of a shadow.
An arm flashes through the reflections,
A breast is outlined with leaves.
Outstretched in the quiet water
The statue of a Goddess slumbers.
But when Autumn comes
The beech leaves cover her with a golden counter-pane.

Balls

Throw the blue ball above the little twigs of the tree-tops,
And cast the yellow ball straight at the buzzing stars.

All our life is a flinging of coloured balls
                to impossible distances.

And in the end what have we?
            A tired arm—a tip-tilted nose.

Ah! Well! Give me the purple one.
Wouldn't it be a fine thing if I could make it stick
On top of the Methodist steeple?

Flotsam

She sat in a Chinese wicker chair
Wide at the top like a spread peacock's tail,
And toyed with a young man's heart which she held
      lightly in her fingers.
She tapped it gently,
Held it up to the sun and looked through it,
Strung it on a chain of seed-pearls and fastened it about
      her neck,
Tossed it into the air and caught it,
Deftly, as though it were a ball.
Before her on the grass sat the young man.
Sometimes he felt an ache where his heart had been.
But he brushed it aside.
He was intent on gazing, and had no time for anything
      else.
Presently she grew tired and handed him back his heart,
But he only laid it on the ground beside him
And went on gazing.

When the maidservant came to tidy up,
She found the heart on the grass.
"What a pretty thing," said the maidservant,
"It is red as a ruby!"
So she picked it up,
And carried it into the house,
And ran a ribbon through it,
And hung it on the looking-glass in her bedroom.
There it hung for many days,
Banging back and forth as the wind blew it.

Misericordia

He earned his bread by making wooden soldiers,
With beautiful golden instruments,
Riding dapple-grey horses.
But when he heard the fanfare of trumpets
And the long rattle of drums
As the army marched out of the city,
He took all his soldiers
And burned them in the grate;
And that night he fashioned a ballet-dancer
Out of tinted tissue-paper,
And the next day he started to carve a Pietà
On the steel hilt
Of a cavalry sword.

Dreams in War Time

I

I wandered through a house of many rooms.
It grew darker and darker,
Until, at last, I could only find my way
By passing my fingers along the wall.
Suddenly my hand shot through an open window,
And the thorn of a rose I could not see
Pricked it so sharply
That I cried aloud.

II

I dug a grave under an oak-tree.
With infinite care, I stamped my spade
Into the heavy grass.
The sod sucked it,
And I drew it out with effort,
Watching the steel run liquid in the moonlight
As it came clear.
I stooped, and dug, and never turned,
For behind me,
On the dried leaves,
My own face lay like a white pebble,
Waiting.

III

I gambled with a silver money.
The dried seed-vessels of "honesty"
Were stacked in front of me.
Dry, white years slipping through my fingers

One by one.
One by one, gathered by the Croupier.
"Faites vos jeux, Messieurs."
I staked on the red,
And the black won.
Dry years,
Dead years;
But I had a system,
I always staked on the red.

IV

I painted the leaves of bushes red
And shouted: "Fire! Fire!"
But the neighbors only laughed.
"We cannot warm our hands at them," they said.
Then they cut down my bushes,
And made a bonfire,
And danced about it.
But I covered my face and wept,
For ashes are not beautiful
Even in the dawn.

V

I followed a procession of singing girls
Who danced to the glitter of tambourines.
Where the street turned at a lighted corner,
I caught the purple dress of one of the dancers,
But, as I grasped it, it tore,
And the purple dye ran from it
Like blood
Upon the ground.

VI

I wished to post a letter,
But although I paid much,
Still the letter was overweight.
"What is in this package?" said the clerk,
"It is very heavy."
"Yes," I said,
"And yet it is only a dried fruit."

VII

I had made a kite,
On it I had pasted golden stars
And white torches,
And the tail was spotted scarlet like a tiger-lily,
And very long.
I flew my kite,
And my soul was contented
Watching it flash against the concave of the sky.
My friends pointed at the clouds;
They begged me to take in my kite.
But I was happy
Seeing the mirror shock of it
Against the black clouds.
Then the lightning came
And struck the kite.
It puffed—blazed—fell.
But still I walked on,
In the drowning rain,
Slowly winding up the string.

Spectacles

He was a landscape architect.

All day he planned Dutch gardens: rectangular, squared
with tulips; Italian gardens: dark with myrtle, thick with
running water; English gardens: prim, box-edged,
espaliered fruit trees flickering on walls, borders of
snap-dragons, pansies, marjoram, rue.

On Saturday afternoons, he did not walk into the coun-
try. He paid a quarter and went to a cinema show, and
gazed—gazed—at marching soldiers, at guns firing
and recoiling, at waste grounds strewn with mutilated
dead. When he took off his glasses, there was moisture
upon them, and his eyes hurt. He could not see to use
a periscope, they said, yet he could draw gardens.

September. 1918

This afternoon was the colour of water falling through
    sunlight;
The trees glittered with the tumbling of leaves;
The sidewalks shone like alleys of dropped maple leaves,
And the houses ran along them laughing out of square,
    open windows.
Under a tree in the park,
Two little boys, lying flat on their faces,

Were carefully gathering red berries
To put in a pasteboard box.

Some day there will be no war,
Then I shall take out this afternoon
And turn it in my fingers,
And remark the sweet taste of it upon my palate,
And note the crisp variety of its flights of leaves.
To-day I can only gather it
And put it into my lunch-box,
For I have time for nothing
But the endeavour to balance myself
Upon a broken world.

Gavotte in D Minor

She wore purple, and when other people slept
She stept lightly—lightly—in her ruby powdered
    slippers
Along the flags of the East portico.
And the moon slowly rifting the heights of cloud
Touched her face so that she bowed
Her head, and held her hand to her eyes
To keep the white shining from her. And she was wise,
For gazing at the moon was like looking on her own
    dead face
Passing alone in a wide place,
Chill and uncosseted, always above
The hot protuberance of life. Love to her
Was morning and a great stir
Of trumpets and tire-women and sharp sun.
As she had begun, so she would end,
Walking alone to the last bend
Where the portico turned the wall.
And her slipper's sound
Was scarce as loud upon the ground
As her tear's fall.
Her long white fingers crisped and clung
Each to each, and her weary tongue
Rattled always the same cold speech:

Gold was not made to lie in grass,
Silver dints at the touch of brass,
The days pass.

Lightly, softly, wearily,
The lady paces, drearily
Listening to the half-shrill croon
Leaves make on a moony Autumn night
When the windy light
Runs over the ivy eerily.
A branch at the corner cocks an obscene eye
As she passes—passes—by, and by—
A hand stretches out from a column's edge,
Faces float in a phosphorent wedge
Through the points of arches, and there is speech
In the carven roof-groins out of reach.
A love-word, a lust-word, shivers and mocks
The placid stroke of the village clocks.
Does the lady hear?
Is any one near?
She jeers at life, must she wed instead
The cold dead?
A marriage-bed of moist green mold,
With an over-head tester of beaten gold.
A splendid price for a splendid scorn,
A tombstone pedigree snarled with thorn
Clouding the letters and the fleur-de-lis,
She will have them in granite for her heart's chill ease.

I set the candle in a draught of air
And watched it swale to the last thin flair.

They laid her in a fair chamber hung with arras,
And they wept her virgin soul.
The arras was woven of the story of Minos and
    Dictynna.
But I grieved that I could no longer hear the shuffle of
    her feet along the portico,
And the ruffling of her train against the stones.

Ch'ang Kan

By Li T'ai-po

When the hair of your Unworthy One first began to
    cover her forehead,
She picked flowers and played in front of the door.
Then you, my Lover, came riding a bamboo horse.
We ran round and round the bed, and tossed about the
    sweetmeats of green plums.
We both lived in the village of Ch'ang Kan.
We were both very young, and knew neither jealousy
    nor suspicion.
At fourteen, I became the wife of my Lord.
I could not yet lay aside my face of shame;
I hung my head, facing the dark wall;
You might call me a thousand times, not once would I
    turn round.
At fifteen, I stopped frowning.
I wanted to be with you, as dust with its ashes.
I often thought that you were the faithful man who
    clung to the bridge-post,
That I should never be obliged to ascend to the
    Looking-for-Husband Ledge.
When I was sixteen, my Lord went far away,

To the Ch'ü T'ang Chasm and the Whirling Water
    Rock of the Yü River
Which, during the Fifth Month, must not be collided
    with;
Where the wailing of the gibbons seems to come from
    the sky.
Your departing footprints are still before the door where
    I bade you good-bye,
In each has sprung up green moss.
The moss is thick, it cannot be swept away.
The leaves are falling, it is early for the Autumn wind to
    blow.
It is the Eighth Month, the butterflies are yellow,
Two are flying among the plants in the West garden;
Seeing them, my heart is bitter with grief, they wound
    the heart of the Unworthy One.
The bloom of my face has faded, sitting with my sorrow.
From early morning until late in the evening, you
    descend the Three Serpent River.
Prepare me first with a letter, bringing me the news of
    when you will reach home.
I will not go far on the road to meet you,
I will go straight until I reach the Long Wind Sands.

Drinking Alone in the Moonlight

By Li T'ai-po

I

A pot of wine among flowers.

I alone, drinking, without a companion.

I lift the cup and invite the bright moon.

My shadow opposite certainly makes us three.

But the moon cannot drink,

And my shadow follows the motions of my body in vain.

For the briefest time are the moon and my shadow my
companions.

Oh, be joyful! One must make the most of Spring.

I sing—the moon walks forward rhythmically;

I dance, and my shadow shatters and becomes confused.

In my waking moments, we are happily blended.

When I am drunk, we are divided from one another and
scattered.

For a long time I shall be obliged to wander without
intention;

But we will keep our appointment by the far-off Cloudy
River.

II

If Heaven did not love wine,

There would be no Wine Star in Heaven.

If Earth did not love wine,

There should be no Wine Springs on Earth.

Why then be ashamed before Heaven to love wine.

I have heard that clear wine is like the Sages;

Again it is said that thick wine is like the Virtuous
   Worthies.
Wherefore it appears that we have swallowed both
   Sages and Worthies.
Why should we strive to be Gods and Immortals?
Three cups, and one can perfectly understand the Great
   Tao;
A gallon, and one is in accord with all nature.
Only those in the midst of it can fully comprehend the
   joys of wine;
I do not proclaim them to the sober.

Descending the Extreme South Mountain; Passing the House of Hu Ssŭ, Lover of Hills; Spending the Night in the Preparation of Wine

By Li T'ai-po

We come down the green-grey jade hill,
The mountain moon accompanies us home.
We turn and look back up the path:
Green, green, the sky; the horizontal, kingfisher-green
   line of the hills is fading.
Holding each other's hands, we reach the house in the
   fields.
Little boys throw open the gate of thorn branches,
The quiet path winds among dark bamboos,
Creepers, bright with new green, brush our garments.
Our words are happy, rest is in them.

Of an excellent flavour, the wine! We scatter the dregs
of it contentedly.
We sing songs for a long time; we chant them to the
wind in the pine-trees.
By the time the songs are finished, the stars in Heaven's
River are few.
I am tipsy. My friend is continuously merry.
In fact, we are so exhilarated that we both forget this
complicated machine, the world.

Autumn River Song
on the Broad Reach
By Li T'ai-po

In the clear green water—the shimmering moon.
In the moonlight—white herons flying.
A young man hears a girl plucking water-chestnuts;
They paddle home together through the night, singing.

Poem Sent on Hearing That Wang Ch'ang-ling Had Been Exiled to Lung Piao
By Li T'ai-po

In Yang Chou, the blossoms are dropping. The night-
jar calls.
I hear it said that you are going to Lung Piao—that you
will cross the Five Streams.

I fling the grief of my heart up to the bright moon
That it may follow the wind and arrive, straight as
      eyesight, to the West of Yeh Lang.

The River Village

By Tu Fu

The river makes a bend and encircles the village with its
      current.
All the long Summer, the affairs and occupations of the
      river village are quiet and simple.
The swallows who nest in the beams go and come as
      they please.
The gulls in the middle of the river enjoy one another,
      they crowd together and touch one another.
My old wife paints a chess-board on paper.
My little sons hammer needles to make fish-hooks.
I have many illnesses, therefore my only necessities are
      medicines;
Besides these, what more can so humble a man as I ask?

The Excursion

A Number of Young Gentlemen of Rank, Accompanied by Singing-Girls, Go Out to Enjoy the Cool of Evening. They Encounter a Shower of Rain

By Tu Fu

I

How delightful, at sunset, to loosen the boat!
A light wind is slow to raise waves.
Deep in the bamboo grove, the guests linger;
The lotus-flowers are pure and bright in the cool
　　evening air.
The young nobles stir the ice-water;
The Beautiful Ones wash the lotus-roots, whose fibres
　　are like silk threads.
A layer of clouds above our heads is black.
It will certainly rain, which impels me to write this
　　poem.

II

The rain comes, soaking the mats upon which we are
　　sitting.
A hurrying wind strikes the bow of the boat.
The rose-red rouge of the ladies from Yüeh is wet;
The Yen beauties are anxious about their kingfisher-
　　eyebrows.
We throw out a rope and draw in to the sloping bank.
　　We tie the boat to the willow-trees.
We roll up the curtains and watch the floating wave-
　　flowers.

Our return is different from our setting out. The wind
    whistles and blows in great gusts.
By the time we reach the shore, it seems as though the
    Fifth Month were Autumn.

Sent to Li Po as a Gift

By Tu Fu

Autumn comes,
We meet each other.
You still whirl about as a thistledown in the wind.
Your Elixir of Immortality is not yet perfected
And, remembering Ko Hung, you are ashamed.
You drink a great deal,
You sing wild songs,
Your days pass in emptiness.
Your nature is a spreading fire,
It is swift and strenuous.
But what does all this bravery amount to?

The Sorceress Gorge

By Tu Fu

Jade dew lies upon the withered and wounded forest of
    maple-trees.
On the Sorceress Hill, over the Sorceress Gorge, the
    mist is desolate and dark.

The ripples of the river increase into waves and blur
with the rapidly flowing sky.
The wind-clouds at the horizon become confused with
the Earth. Darkness.
The myriad chrysanthemums have bloomed twice. Days
to come—tears.
The solitary little boat is moored, but my heart is in the
old-time garden.
Everywhere people are hastening to measure and cut
out their Winter clothes.
At sunset, in the high City of the White Emperor, the
hurried pounding of washed garments.

Together We Know Happiness

Written by a Descendant of the Founder of the Southern T'ang Dynasty

Silent and alone, I ascended the West Cupola.
The moon was like a golden hook.
In the quiet, empty, inner courtyard, the coolness of
early Autumn enveloped the wu-t'ung tree.

Scissors cannot cut this thing;
Unravelled, it joins again and clings.
It is the sorrow of separation,
And none other tastes to the heart like this.

Songs of the Courtesans

(Written During the Liang Dynasty)

Ai Ai Thinks of the Man She Loves

How often must I pass the moonlight nights alone?
I gaze far—far—for the Seven Scents Chariot.
My girdle drops because my waist is shrunken.
The golden hairpins of my disordered head-dress are all
      askew.

After How Many Years

Autumn

Hoar-frost is falling,
And the water of the river runs clear.
The moon has not yet risen,
But there are many stars.
I hear the watch-dogs
In the near-by village.
On the opposite bank
Autumn lamps are burning in the windows.
I am sick,
Sick with all the illnesses there are.
I can bear this cold no longer,
And a great pity for my whole past life
Fills my mind.
The boat has started at last.
O be careful not to run foul
Of the fishing-nets!

Winter

I was lonely in the cold valleys
Where I was stationed.
But I am still lonely,
And when no one is near
I sigh.
My gluttonous wife rails at me
To guard her bamboo shoots.
My son is ill and neglects to water
The flowers.
Oh yes,
Old red rice can satisfy hunger,
And poor people can buy muddy, unstrained wine
On credit.
But the pile of land-tax bills
Is growing;
I will go over and see my neighbour,
Leaning on my staff.

Li Hai-ku, 19th Century

Merely Statement

You sent me a sprig of mignonette,
Cool-coloured, quiet, and it was wet
With green sea-spray, and the salt and the sweet
Mingled to a fragrance weary and discreet
As a harp played softly in a great room at sunset.

You said: "My sober mignonette
Will brighten your room and you will not forget."

But I have pressed your flower and laid it away
In a letter, tied with a ribbon knot.
I have not forgot.
But there is a passion-flower in my vase
Standing above a close-cleared space
In the midst of a jumble of papers and books.
The passion-flower holds my eyes,
And the light-under-light of its blue and purple dyes
Is a hot surprise.
How then can I keep my looks
From the passion-flower leaning sharply over the books?
When one has seen
The difficult magnificence of a queen
On one's table,

Is one able
To observe any colour in a mignonette?
I will not think of sunset, I crave the dawn,
With its rose-red light on the wings of a swan,
And a queen pacing slowly through the Parthenon,
Her dress a stare of purple between pillars of stone.

Vespers

Last night, at sunset,
The foxgloves were like tall altar candles.
Could I have lifted you to the roof of the greenhouse,
    my Dear,
I should have understood their burning.

White Currants

Shall I give you white currants?
I do not know why, but I have a sudden fancy for this
    fruit.
At the moment, the idea of them cherishes my senses,
And they seem more desirable than flawless emeralds.
Since I am, in fact, empty-handed,
I might have chosen gems out of India,
But I choose white currants.
Is it because the raucous wind is hurtling round the
    house-corners?

I see it with curled lips and stripped fangs, gaunt with a
    hunting energy,
Come to snout, and nibble, and kill the little crocus roots.
Shall we call it white currants?
You may consider it as a symbol if you please.
You may find them tart, or sweet, or merely agreeable in
    colour,
So long as you accept them,
And me.

Afterglow

Peonies
The strange pink colour of Chinese porcelains;
Wonderful—the glow of them.
But, my Dear, it is the pale blue larkspur
Which swings windily against my heart.
Other Summers—
And a cricket chirping in the grass.

Lilacs

Lilacs,
False blue,
White,
Purple,
Colour of lilac,

Your great puffs of flowers
Are everywhere in this my New England.
Among your heart-shaped leaves
Orange orioles hop like music-box birds and sing
Their little weak soft songs;
In the crooks of your branches
The bright eyes of song sparrows sitting on spotted eggs
Peer restlessly through the light and shadow
Of all Springs.
Lilacs in dooryards
Holding quiet conversations with an early moon;
Lilacs watching a deserted house
Settling sideways into the grass of an old road;
Lilacs, wind-beaten, staggering under a lopsided shock
    of bloom
Above a cellar dug into a hill.
You are everywhere.
You were everywhere.
You tapped the window when the preacher preached his
    sermon,
And ran along the road beside the boy going to school.
You stood by pasture-bars to give the cows good milking,
You persuaded the housewife that her dish pan was of
    silver
And her husband an image of pure gold.
You flaunted the fragrance of your blossoms
Through the wide doors of Custom Houses—
You, and sandal-wood, and tea,
Charging the noses of quill-driving clerks
When a ship was in from China.
You called to them: "Goose-quill men, goose-quill men,

May is a month for flitting,"
Until they writhed on their high stools
And wrote poetry on their letter-sheets behind the
    propped-up ledgers.
Paradoxical New England clerks,
Writing inventories in ledgers, reading the "Song of
    Solomon" at night,
So many verses before bed-time,
Because it was the Bible.
The dead fed you
Amid the slant stones of graveyards.
Pale ghosts who planted you
Came in the night-time
And let their thin hair blow through your clustered
    stems.
You are of the green sea,
And of the stone hills which reach a long distance.
You are of elm-shaded streets with little shops where
    they sell kites and marbles,
You are of great parks where everyone walks and no-
    body is at home.
You cover the blind sides of greenhouses
And lean over the top to say a hurry-word through the
    glass
To your friends, the grapes, inside.

Lilacs,
False blue,
White,
Purple,
Colour of lilac,

You have forgotten your Eastern origin,
The veiled women with eyes like panthers,
The swollen, aggressive turbans of jewelled Pashas.
Now you are a very decent flower,
A reticent flower,
A curiously clear-cut, candid flower,
Standing beside clean doorways,
Friendly to a house-cat and a pair of spectacles,
Making poetry out of a bit of moonlight
And a hundred or two sharp blossoms.

Maine knows you,
Has for years and years;
New Hampshire knows you,
And Massachusetts
And Vermont.
Cape Cod starts you along the beaches to Rhode Island;
Connecticut takes you from a river to the sea.
You are brighter than apples,
Sweeter than tulips,
You are the great flood of our souls
Bursting above the leaf-shapes of our hearts,
You are the smell of all Summers,
The love of wives and children,
The recollection of the gardens of little children,
You are State Houses and Charters
And the familiar treading of the foot to and fro on a
    road it knows.
May is lilac here in New England,
May is a thrush singing "Sun up!" on a tip-top ash-tree,
May is white clouds behind pine-trees

Puffed out and marching upon a blue sky.
May is a green as no other,
May is much sun through small leaves,
May is soft earth,
And apple-blossoms,
And windows open to a South wind.
May is a full light wind of lilac
From Canada to Narragansett Bay.

Lilacs,
False blue,
White,
Purple,
Colour of lilac.
Heart-leaves of lilac all over New England,
Roots of lilac under all the soil of New England,
Lilac in me because I am New England,
Because my roots are in it,
Because my leaves are of it,
Because my flowers are for it,
Because it is my country
And I speak to it of itself
And sing of it with my own voice
Since certainly it is mine.

Meeting-House Hill

I must be mad, or very tired,
When the curve of a blue bay beyond a railroad track
Is shrill and sweet to me like the sudden springing of a
    tune,
And the sight of a white church above thin trees in a city
    square
Amazes my eyes as though it were the Parthenon.
Clear, reticent, superbly final,
With the pillars of its portico refined to a cautious
    elegance,
It dominates the weak trees,
And the shot of its spire
Is cool, and candid,
Rising into an unresisting sky.
Strange meeting-house
Pausing a moment upon a squalid hill-top.
I watch the spire sweeping the sky,
I am dizzy with the movement of the sky,
I might be watching a mast
With its royals set full
Straining before a two-reef breeze.
I might be sighting a tea-clipper,
Tacking into the blue bay,
Just back from Canton
With her hold full of green and blue porcelain,
And a Chinese coolie leaning over the rail
Gazing at the white spire
With dull, sea-spent eyes.

The Sisters

Taking us by and large, we're a queer lot
We women who write poetry. And when you think
How few of us there've been, it's queerer still.
I wonder what it is that makes us do it,
Singles us out to scribble down, man-wise,
The fragments of ourselves. Why are we
Already mother-creatures, double-bearing,
With matrices in body and in brain?
I rather think that there is just the reason
We are so sparse a kind of human being;
The strength of forty thousand Atlases
Is needed for our every-day concerns.
There's Sapho, now I wonder what was Sapho.
I know a single slender thing about her:
That, loving, she was like a burning birch-tree
All tall and glittering fire, and that she wrote
Like the same fire caught up to Heaven and held there,
A frozen blaze before it broke and fell.
Ah, me! I wish I could have talked to Sapho,
Surprised her reticences by flinging mine
Into the wind. This tossing off of garments
Which cloud the soul is none too easy doing
With us to-day. But still I think with Sapho
One might accomplish it, were she in the mood
To bare her loveliness of words and tell
The reasons, as she possibly conceived them,
Of why they are so lovely. Just to know
How she came at them, just to watch
The crisp sea sunshine playing on her hair,

And listen, thinking all the while 'twas she
Who spoke and that we two were sisters
Of a strange, isolated little family.
And she is Sapho—Sapho—not Miss or Mrs.,
A leaping fire we call so for convenience;
But Mrs. Browning—who would ever think
Of such presumption as to call her "Ba."
Which draws the perfect line between sea-cliffs
And a close-shuttered room in Wimpole Street.
Sapho could fly her impulses like bright
Balloons tip-tilting to a morning air
And write about it. Mrs. Browning's heart
Was squeezed in stiff conventions. So she lay
Stretched out upon a sofa, reading Greek
And speculating, as I must suppose,
In just this way on Sapho; all the need,
The huge, imperious need of loving, crushed
Within the body she believed so sick.
And it was sick, poor lady, because words
Are merely simulacra after deeds
Have wrought a pattern; when they take the place
Of actions they breed a poisonous miasma
Which, though it leave the brain, eats up the body.
So Mrs. Browning, aloof and delicate,
Lay still upon her sofa, all her strength
Going to uphold her over-topping brain.
It seems miraculous, but she escaped
To freedom and another motherhood
Than that of poems. She was a very woman
And needed both.
            If I had gone to call,

Would Wimpole Street have been the kindlier place,
Or Casa Guidi, in which to have met her?
I am a little doubtful of that meeting,
For Queen Victoria was very young and strong
And all-pervading in her apogee
At just that time. If we had struck to poetry,
Sternly refusing to be drawn off by mesmerism
Or Roman revolutions, it might have done.
For, after all, she is another sister,
But always, I rather think, an older sister
And not herself so curious a technician
As to admit newfangled modes of writing—
"Except, of course, in Robert, and that is neither
Here nor there for Robert is a genius."
I do not like the turn this dream is taking,
Since I am very fond of Mrs. Browning
And very much indeed should like to hear her
Graciously asking me to call her "Ba."
But then the Devil of Verisimilitude
Creeps in and forces me to know she wouldn't.
Convention again, and how it chafes my nerves,
For we are such a little family
Of singing sisters, and as if I didn't know
What those years felt like tied down to the sofa.
Confound Victoria, and the slimy inhibitions
She loosed on all us Anglo-Saxon creatures!
Suppose there hadn't been a Robert Browning,
No "Sonnets from the Portuguese" would have been
        written.
They are the first of all her poems to be,
One might say, fertilized. For, after all,

A poet is flesh and blood as well as brain
And Mrs. Browning, as I said before,
Was very, very woman. Well, there are two
Of us, and vastly unlike that's for certain.
Unlike at least until we tear the veils
Away which commonly gird souls. I scarcely think
Mrs. Browning would have approved the process
In spite of what had surely been relief;
For speaking souls must always want to speak
Even when bat-eyed, narrow-minded Queens
Set prudishness to keep the keys of impulse.
Then do the frowning Gods invent new banes
And make the need of sofas. But Sapho was dead
And I, and others, not yet peeped above
The edge of possibility. So that's an end
To speculating over tea-time talks
Beyond the movement of pentameters
With Mrs. Browning.
                                 But I go dreaming on,
In love with these my spiritual relations.
I rather think I see myself walk up
A flight of wooden steps and ring a bell
And send a card in to Miss Dickinson.
Yet that's a very silly way to do.
I should have taken the dream twist-ends about
And climbed over the fence and found her deep
Engrossed in the doings of a humming-bird
Among nasturtiums. Not having expected strangers,
She might forget to think me one, and holding up
A finger say quite casually: "Take care.
Don't frighten him, he's only just begun."

"Now this," I will believe I should have thought,
"Is even better than Sapho. With Emily
You're really here, or never anywhere at all
In range of mind." Wherefore, having begun
In this strict centre, we could slowly progress
To various circumferences, as we pleased.
We could, but should we? That would quite depend
On Emily. I think she'd be exacting,
Without intention possibly, and ask
A thousand tight-rope tricks of understanding.
But, bless you, I would somersault all day
If by so doing I might stay with her.
I hardly think that we should mention souls
Although they might just round the corner from us
In some half-quizzical, half-wistful metaphor.
I'm very sure that I should never seek
To turn her parables to stated fact.
Sapho would speak, I think, quite openly,
And Mrs. Browning guard a careful silence,
But Emily would set doors ajar and slam them
And love you for your speed of observation.

Strange trio of my sisters, most diverse,
And how extraordinarily unlike
Each is to me, and which way shall I go?
Sapho spent and gained; and Mrs. Browning,
After a miser girlhood, cut the strings
Which tied her money-bags and let them run;
But Emily hoarded—hoarded—only giving
Herself to cold, white paper. Starved and tortured,
She cheated her despair with games of patience

And fooled herself by winning. Frail little elf,
The lonely brain-child of a gaunt maturity,
She hung her womanhood upon a bough
And played ball with the stars—too long—too long—
The garment of herself hung on a tree
Until at last she lost even the desire
To take it down. Whose fault? Why let us say,
To be consistent, Queen Victoria's.
But really, not to over-rate the queen,
I feel obliged to mention Martin Luther,
And behind him the long line of Church Fathers
Who draped their prurience like a dirty cloth
About the naked majesty of God.
Good-bye, my sisters, all of you are great,
And all of you are marvellously strange,
And none of you has any word for me.
I cannot write like you, I cannot think
In terms of Pagan or of Christian now.
I only hope that possibly some day
Some other woman with an itch for writing
May turn to me as I have turned to you
And chat with me a brief few minutes. How
We lie, we poets! It is three good hours
I have been dreaming. Has it seemed so long
To you? And yet I thank you for the time
Although you leave me sad and self-distrustful,
For older sisters are very sobering things.
Put on your cloaks, my dears, the motor's waiting.
No, you have not seemed strange to me, but near,
Frightfully near, and rather terrifying.
I understand you all, for in myself—

Is that presumption? Yet indeed it's true—
We are one family. And still my answer
Will not be any one of yours, I see.
Well, never mind that now. Good night! Good night!

Nuit Blanche

I want no horns to rouse me up to-night,
And trumpets make too clamorous a ring
To fit my mood, it is so weary white
I have no wish for doing any thing.

A music coaxed from humming strings would please;
Not plucked, but drawn in creeping cadences
Across a sunset wall where some Marquise
Picks a pale rose amid strange silences.

Ghostly and vaporous her gown sweeps by
The twilight dusking wall, I hear her feet
Delaying on the gravel, and a sigh,
Briefly permitted, touches the air like sleet.

And it is dark, I hear her feet no more.
A red moon leers beyond the lily-tank.
A drunken moon ogling a sycamore,
Running long fingers down its shining flank.

A lurching moon, as nimble as a clown,
Cuddling the flowers and trees which burn like glass

Red, kissing lips, I feel you on my gown—
Kiss me, red lips, and then pass—pass.

Music, you are pitiless to-night.
And I so old, so cold, so languorously white.

Orientation

When the young ladies of the boarding-school take the
    air,
They walk in pairs, each holding a blush-red parasol
    against the sun.
From my window they look like an ambulating parterre
Of roses, I cannot tell one from one.

There is a certain young person I dream of by night,
And paint by day on little two-by-three inch squares
Of ivory. Which is she? Which of all the parasols in sight
Covers the blithe, mocking face which stares
At me from twenty miniatures, confusing the singleness
    of my delight?
You know my window well enough—the fourth from
    the corner. Oh, you know.
Slant your parasol a bit this way, if you please,
And take for yourself the very correct bow
I make toward the line of demure young ladies
Perambulating the street in a neat row.
It is true I have never seen beneath your parasol,
Therefore my miniatures resemble one another not at all.

You must pick yourself like a button-hole bouquet,
And lift the parasol to my face one day,
And let me see you laughing at the sun—
Or at me. Then I will choose the one
Of my twenty miniatures most like you
And destroy the others, with which I shall have nothing
more to do.

The Humming-birds

Up—up—water shooting,
Jet of water, white and silver,
Tinkling with the morning sun-bells.
Red as sun-blood, whizz of fire,
Shock of fire-spray and water.
It is the humming-birds flying against the stream of the
fountain.
The trumpet-vine bursts into a scatter of humming-
birds,
The scarlet-throated trumpet flowers explode with
humming-birds.
The fountain waits to toss them diamonds.
I clasp my hands over my heart
Which will not let loose its humming-birds,
Which will not break to green and ruby,
Which will not let its wings touch air.
Pound and hammer me with irons,
Crack me so that flame can enter,
Pull me open, loose the thunder

Of wings within me.
Leave me wrecked and consoled,
A maker of humming-birds
Who dare bathe in a leaping water.

The Sand Altar

With a red grain and a blue grain, placed in precisely
the proper positions, I made a beautiful god, with
plumes of yard-long feathers and a swivel eye.

And with a red grain and a blue grain, placed in pre-
cisely the proper positions, I made a dragon, with
scaly wings and a curling, iniquitous tail.

Then I reflected:
If, with the same materials, I can make both god and
dragon, of what use is the higher mathematics?

Having said this, I went outdoors and stood under a tree
and listened to the frogs singing their evening songs
in the green darkness.

Time-Web

The day is sharp and hurried
As wind upon a dahlia stem;
It is harsh and abrupt with me
As a North-east breeze
Striking a bed of sunflowers.
Why should I break at the root
And cast all my fragile flowers in the dust—
I who am no taller than a creeping pansy?
I should be sturdy and definite,
Yet am I tossed, and agitated, and pragmatically bending.

Katydids

Shore of Lake Michigan

Katydids scraped in the dim trees,
And I thought they were little white skeletons
Playing the fiddle with a pair of finger-bones.

How long is it since Indians walked here,
Stealing along the sands with smooth feet?
How long is it since Indians died here
And the creeping sands scraped them bone from bone?
Dead Indians under the sands, playing their bones
     against strings of wampum.
The roots of new, young trees have torn their graves
     asunder,
But in the branches sit little white skeletons
Rasping a bitter death-dirge through the August night.

Eleonora Duse

I

Seeing's believing, so the ancient word
Chills buds to shrivelled powder flecks, turns flax
To smoky heaps of straw whose small flames wax
Only to gasp and die. The thing's absurd!
Have blind men ever seen or deaf men heard?
What one beholds but measures what one lacks.
Where is the prism to draw gold from blacks,
Or flash the iris colours of a bird?
Not in the eye, be sure, nor in the ear,
Nor in an instrument of twisted glass,
Yet there are sights I see and sounds I hear
Which ripple me like water as they pass.
This that I give you for a dear love's sake
Is curling noise of waves marching along a lake.

II

A letter or a poem—the words are set
To either tune. Be careful how you slice
The flap which is held down by this device
Impressed upon it. In one moment met
A cameo, intaglio, a fret
Of workmanship, and I. Like melted ice
I took the form and froze so, turned precise
And brittle seal, a creed in silhouette.
Seeing's believing? What then would you see?
A chamfered dragon? Three spear-heads of steel?
A motto done in flowered charactry?
The thin outline of Mercury's winged heel?

Look closer, do you see a name, a face,
Or just a cloud dropped down before a holy place?

III

Lady, to whose enchantment I took shape
So long ago, though carven to your grace,
Bearing, like quickened wood, your sweet sad face
Cut in my flesh, yet may I not escape
My limitations: words that jibe and gape
After your loveliness and make grimace
And travesty where they should interlace
The weave of sun-spun ocean round a cape.
Pictures then must contain you, this and more,
The sigh of wind floating on ripe June hay,
The desolate pulse of snow beyond a door,
The grief of mornings seen as yesterday.
All that you are mingles as one sole cry
To point a world aright which is so much awry.

IV

If Beauty set her image on a stage
And bid it mirror moments so intense
With passion and swift largess of the sense
To a divine exactness, stamp a page
With mottoes of hot blood, and disengage
No atom of mankind's experience,
But lay the soul's complete incontinence
Bare while it tills grief's gusty acreage.
Doing this, you, spon-image to her needs,
She picked to pierce, reveal, and soothe again,
Shattering by means of you the tinsel creeds

Offered as meat to the pinched hearts of men.
So, sacrificing you, she fed those others
Who bless you in their prayers even before their mothers.

V

Life seized you with her iron hands and shook
The fire of your boundless burning out
To fall on us, poor little ragged rout
Of common men, till like a flaming book
We, letters of a message, flashed and took
The fiery flare of prophecy, devout
Torches to bear your oil, a dazzling shout,
The liquid golden running of a brook.
Who, being upborne on racing streams of light,
Seeing new heavens sprung from dusty hells,
Considered you, and what might be your plight,
Robbed, plundered—since Life's cruel plan compels
The perfect sacrifice of one great soul
To make a myriad others even a whit more whole.

VI

Seeing you stand once more before my eyes
In your pale dignity and tenderness,
Wearing your frailty like a misty dress
Draped over the great glamour which denies
To years their domination, all disguise
Time can achieve is but to add a stress,
A finer fineness, as though some caress
Touched you a moment to a strange surprise.
Seeing you after these long lengths of years,
I only know the glory come again,

A majesty bewildered by my tears,
A golden sun spangling slant shafts of rain,
Moonlight delaying by a sick man's bed,
A rush of daffodils where wastes of dried leaves spread.

The Doll

You know, my Dear, I have a way, each Summer
When leaves have changed from ecstasies in green
To something like a crowd with raised umbrellas
Pushing for places at a theatre door,
Whenever there's a reasonable wind—
And when there isn't, why I think it's worse,
They droop so underneath the copper sun
Sitting upon them like a metal cover;
I think the trees look positively tired
Holding the mass of them up all the time.
Well, as I say, when every breeze is smothered
By heavy, lagging leaves on dusty trees,
And all I smell is asphalt and hot tar,
And motor horns destroy the moonlight nights,
I pack myself, and some stray sheets of music,
Into a train and hie me to South Norton.
I came from there, and little drowsy town
Although it is, I still go back (or used to)
And find it with a narrow odd contentment
As grey and glistening as it always was,
Some of it painted, some a silver shimmer
Of weathered clapboards melting to decay.
There always is a blaze of Summer flowers
Cramming the dooryards—stocks and portulaca,

And golden glow above the first floor windows,
And China asters mixed with marigolds.
White paint looks very well indeed behind them
And green blinds, always down, you understand,
South Norton people will not risk the daylight
Upon their best room furniture, and really
When you possess an inlaid teak-wood table,
With mother-of-pearl and ebony in squares,
And on it, set precisely in their order,
Stand ivory chess-men, red and white, the queens
A pair of ancient Maharanies copied
To every quaintness of their grand attire
And not a button or embroidery
Skimped by the Hindu carver; when your chairs
Are waxed as never chair is waxed to-day,
And there are corners lit by golden silks,
And mandarin fruit-dishes in high glass cupboards,
Perhaps you may at least be half forgiven
For only opening the room for weddings
Or when some guest from Boston comes to call.
I have called often in such drawing-rooms,
Confused at first by coming from the dazzle
Of a white August sea, and almost groping
To find my hostess in the green-blind dusk,
While all the time my nose was being grateful
For the great puffs of pot-pourri and cloves,
The gusts of myrrh, and sandalwood, and ginger
Invisibly progressing up and down.
These scented rooms are just a paraphrase
Of something penetrant, but never clear,
Never completely taken nor rejected,

Unrealized flotsam of the tides of trade;
And these frail, ancient ladies are like tea-dust
Left in the bottom of a painted chest,
Poor fluttering souls, surrounded by their "things,"
Oblivious of the sea which brought them here.
My Dear, I prose, you really must not let me,
For after all I have something to say.
I never make these duty calls until
My music lessons are a week away
And each day's mail is stuffed with pupil's letters
Asking for dates and prices, then I go
The rounds and drink a dish of tea with each
Old fragile chrysalis and so come home.
For many years I've always ended up
With the two Misses Perkins. They were a whiff
Of eighteen-forty, and I rather liked
To talk to them and then come back and play
Debussy, and thank God I had read Freud;
The contrast was as genial as curry.
I only wish that I could make you see them,
Their garden path with spice-bushes and lilacs,
The scraper by the door, the polished knocker,
And then the hall with the model of a clipper
Upon a table in a square glass case.
She is a replica of the "Flying Dolphin"
And Captain Perkins made her on a voyage
Of eighteen months to China and Ceylon,
Miss Julia just remembers when he brought
The model home and put it where it stands.
I always laid my gloves upon the table
Just by the clipper's stern, and stood my sunshade

Against the corner, and tiptoed up the stairs.
Miss Perkins was an invalid, for years
She had not left her bed, so I was summoned
Up slippery stairs and over cool, long matting
Into her room, and there in a great four-poster
The little lady would greet me with effusion.
"Clara, Dear, how good of you to come,
Julia and I were wondering if you would.
You'll have a cake and a small glass of sherry.
Hannah will bring them in directly. Now
How is the music getting on? To think
You play at concerts! Julia and I read
About your triumphs in the newspapers."
And all the time, behind the house, the sea
was moving—moving—with a long, slow sound.
I could not hear it, but I clung to it,
For naturally this room looked on the street.
It was a pretty room with bright glazed chintz,
And Naples bay in staring blue gouache,
Flanked by Vesuvius at night, both pictures framed
In peeling gold. Upon the mantelpiece
Were silhouettes: the Captain and his wife,
Miss Perkins and Miss Julia in pantalettes,
A China bear for matches, and a clock
Suspended between alabaster pillars.
But what I never could keep long from seeing
Was a large wax doll, dressed in the Paris fashion
Of sixty years ago, with a lace tippet
And much-flounced skirt over a crinoline,
Upright in a winged arm-chair by the bed.
She sat and gazed with an uncanny ardour

Straight at the andiron, her hands palms upward,
Her feet in heelless slippers wide apart.
She fascinated me. Those blue glass eyes
Had an unearthly meaning, staring straight
Before her in her faded finery.
I had to draw a chair up from the wall,
For never did Miss Perkins or Miss Julia
Suggest that I should sit in the winged chair.
I found my mind all drawn upon a focus,
I thought wax doll and very nearly said so,
And I am very much afraid I missed the point
Of one or two quite artless little sallies.
They never said a word, and I with rigour
Suppressed my curiosity and merely listened
With sometimes half a mind and sometimes none.
I drank the sherry and I eat the cake,
I kissed Miss Perkins when I came to go,
Bending over the bed, my skirt just touching
The doll, I think, and then the call was over.
Of course at first the thing made no impression.
I thought they had been clearing out the attic
And come upon the doll; but when each year
She was still sitting there, I grew to dread
Encountering her, she seemed so full of tales,
Tell-tales of maiden ladies left alone
With still things on the walls and mantelpieces
And nothing moving round them but the sea
Kept out of reach beyond the matted entry.
One year, in early April, coming in
All flushed with having played Moussorgski's "Pictures"
To an enthusiastic audience,

I found a black-edged letter on my table,
Miss Julia writing that "Dear Sister Jane
Had passed away, she wanted me to know."
The words were quaintly quiet and resigned,
The slim and pointed writing very calm,
But still there seemed a wistful hint of dread.
I knew, in fact, Miss Julia was alone.
I wrote—oh, what one always writes, the things
One does not think, and does not want to think.
I sent the letter, and the answer came
As slim, and pointed, and reticent as ever.
And that was all until I reached South Norton.
Of course I went at once to see Miss Julia.
She greeted me beside the clipper-ship,
And there was something grim about that vessel
Placidly sailing on its painted waves
With coffins passing through the door beside it,
From time to time, while nothing ever came.
I wondered what would be its fate, some junk-shop
Probably, when Miss Julia too had gone.
Poor soul, she seemed to flicker with excitement
And sorrow all in one. The great importance
Of doing something which was not commanded
Appeared in vague authoritative gestures
Which seemed but half controlled and faded off
Into a quiver of movement so pathetic
It made me want to cry. She begged me
To go upstairs. "I cannot bear to be
In any other room but Jane's," she told me.
"I've sat there so much with her, quite ten years
It was she did not leave it." So we mounted

The broad old stairs, and softly trod the matting,
Walking gently as in a house of mourning.
I was resentful, it was four full months
Since I had got that lonely little letter.
Was this a mausoleum? Was Miss Julia
To find her only company with ghosts?
The gaudy paper of the narrow hallway,
Flushing its minarets to a sapphire Heaven
Seemed to be mocking us with Eastern splendour,
With Eastern customs and an Eastern languor.
The conch shells roared a siren song of oceans,
Flanking the newel posts, as we passed by them.
Miss Jane's room was a lovely blaze of sunlight,
The empty bed was orderly and sane,
The Bay of Naples gladdened without hurting.
I shook myself free of the swarming stillness
And saw with satisfaction that the chair,
The doll chair, had been moved, it stood beside
The window with its back toward the room.
Why did I walk up to it? I don't know.
Some feeling that the usualness of streets
Comes kindly over a long spent emotion
Perhaps. At any rate, I did so, saying
How bright and gay the portulacas were,
Or something of the sort. And then I started
To sit down in the chair and saw the doll
With palms stretched out and little slippered feet
Pointing before her. There she sat, her eyes
Fixed glassily upon the window-pane.
I may have jumped, at any rate Miss Julia
Flushing a painful pink said steadily:

"It was so dull for her after Jane died,
I moved her here where she could see the street.
It's very comforting to watch the passing,
I think. I always find it so." That's all,
I don't know how the visit went, nor what
I said, nor where I sat. I only know
I took the train that evening back to town
And stayed up half the night playing Stravinsky.
I dreamt wax doll for three weeks afterwards,
And I shall go to London this vacation.

To a Lady of Undeniable Beauty and Practised Charm

No peacock strutting on a balustrade
Could air his feathers with a cooler grace,
Assume a finer insolence of pace,
Or make his sole advance a cavalcade
Of sudden shifts of colour, slants of shade,
Than you, the cold indifference of your face
Sharpening the cunning lure of velvets, lace,
Greens, blues, and golds, seduction on parade.
You take the accolade of staring eyes
As something due your elegance of pose,
Feeding your vanity on pecks of dust,
The weary iteration which supplies
No zest. I see you as a cankered rose
Its silver petals curled and cracked with rust.

Caustic

Certainly you gave me your heart,
I don't in the least deny it.
And a splendid heart it was,
Of white sea jade strewn over with ochre shadings and
      polished to the tip touch of brilliance.
I strung it on my watch-chain.
But then, I seldom wear a watch nowadays;
I do not need it to tell that the black sun
Is sinking into a sea of garnet flame.

Carrefour

O you,
Who came upon me once
Stretched under apple-trees just after bathing,
Why did you not strangle me before speaking
Rather than fill me with the wild white honey of your
      words
And then leave me to the mercy
Of the forest bees.

Granadilla

I cut myself upon the thought of you
And yet I come back to it again and again.
A kind of fury makes me want to draw you out

From the dimness of the present
And set you sharply above me in a wheel of roses.
Then, going obviously to inhale their fragrance,
I touch the blade of you and cling upon it,
And only when the blood runs out across my fingers
Am I at all satisfied.

Threnody

On an evening of black snow
I walked along the causeway,
Wishing that I too might melt
Between the agitated fingers
Of a stuttering, intolerable sea.

After an Illness

To a Cat from whom one has been separated for a long time

I have come back, Winky.
After a long time—yes.
There was a heavy sodden sea,
And I in the midst of it.
Before me, white snakes swam in a slime of seaweed.
They drew their bodies through the seaweed with a
        dreadful rustle
Like dead leaves on sand,

And left long open lanes behind them
Which glowed a clotted purple
Under the rays of a bursting, half-sunk sun.
Somewhere, on the right, were shores
With high glass cliffs.
The cliffs were hot and leapt up and down unceasingly,
And the heat from them blistered my body
Even under the water as I swam.
A wind rose
And drove the weeds faster upon me,
And I struggled in fear of the snakes who came swiftly—
    swiftly—
Then I sank down somewhere out of the sea
Into a place of mist.
I was blind,
But my ears were shrunken points of awareness,
I was anguished by the keenness of my ears,
For all round were loud voices
Shouting harsh, unintelligible things
Which I strove to understand, but could not.
I trod upon the voices,
But they shifted like pebbles beneath my feet.
I fought with them,
Flinging them from me,
Pushing them down with my hands.
At last I had them under me as I was rising—
I saw nothing, but I was rising—
Then my mouth choked with salt,
And the salt entered my eyes and unsealed them.
Light was an explosion in my brain,

And I floated again in the seaweed sea
Under the bloody cliffs which leapt like flame.

Now I am sitting in a room again,
With fire-light fluttering on the walls
And you in my lap—purring.
Little cat, are you as glad to have me to lie upon
As I am to feel your fur under my hand?
Your purr sounds like the blowing of feathers in a wind;
It is a strangely comfortable sound,
And there is no other,
For the night smiles and says nothing.

The Mirror

Opaque because of the run mercury at its back,
White with a breath of yellow, like tarnished silver,
The old mirror hangs over the chimney-piece
Incased in its carved frame, and reflects the room
    beneath.
It is warped and bulging, because of the great fires
Of other years; and dim with the sun shining in it every
    Spring.
Old men and children move before it, and it reflects
    them all,
Pulling them this way and that in its uneven surface.
The pictures pass over it like mist over a morning window,
And it hangs in its carved frame, tarnished and beautiful,
And reflects everything.

New Heavens for Old

I am useless.
What I do is nothing,
What I think has no savour.
There is an almanac between the windows:
It is of the year when I was born.

My fellows call to me to join them,
They shout for me,
Passing the house in a great wind of vermilion banners.
They are fresh and fulminant,
They are indecent and strut with the thought of it,
They laugh, and curse, and brawl,
And cheer a holocaust of "Who comes first!" at the iron
    fronts of the houses at the two edges of the street.
Young men with naked hearts jeering between iron
    house-fronts,
Young men with naked bodies beneath their clothes
Passionately conscious of them,
Ready to strip off their clothes,
Ready to strip off their customs, their usual routine,
Clamouring for the rawness of life,
In love with appetite,
Proclaiming it as a creed,
Worshipping youth,
Worshipping themselves.
They call for women and the women come,
They bare the whiteness of their lusts to the dead gaze
    of the old house-fronts,

They roar down the street like flame,
They explode upon the dead houses like new, sharp fire.

But I—
I arrange three roses in a Chinese vase:
A pink one,
A red one,
A yellow one.
I fuss over their arrangement.
Then I sit in a South window
And sip pale wine with a touch of hemlock in it,
And think of Winter nights,
And field-mice crossing and re-crossing
The spot which will be my grave.

Anecdote

First Soliloquy

Her breasts were small, upright, virginal;
Even through her clothes I could feel the nipples
      pointing upward when I touched her inadvertently.
The chastity of her garments was pronounced,
But no disposal of material could keep the shape of her
      breasts unseen.

And you would walk as a Spring wind,
You would order your demeanour as though there were
      still frost in the air,

You would keep me to my distance by the cool agree-
    ableness of your speech.
You are foolish, Madam, or deceived.
Is it possible you underrate my sensibility
And do not realize that I hold your breasts
In the hollow of my hand?

Second Soliloquy

His voice was a dagger tipped with honey,
His touch a scimitar dripping myrrh and gall.
He parted me from myself
And I stood alone in sunshine and trembled.
I caught my garments about me,
But they withered one by one as leaves wither, and fell.
I was alone in the wide sunlight;
His eyes were winds which would not leave me.
I would have sought a tree,
But the place where I was was bare and light.
Merciless light he shed upon me,
And I stretched my arms in shame and rejoicing.
Why do you stand there watching me?
Are you blind to what is really happening
That you talk so lightly of trifles?
Stop talking, you suffocate me.
Does any one notice?
Why do you strip me before all these people—
You, who care nothing for my nakedness?
Unbearable the anguish of my body,
The ache of my breasts,
The strain of covering myself is choking me.

Why do you do nothing but talk?
Have you no hands, no heart,
Or are you so cynical that you expose me for a whim?
Oh, I am well-trained, be sure of that,
But can you not see through my pretense?
It is agony to hold myself away from you,
Yet you are as impassive as a stone Hermes before
      whom Venus herself would need no cloak.
Now that you are gone, what have you left me?
No privacy at all, I think.
You have stolen my secrecy, and flung it back as some-
      thing not worth taking.
I have only the harsh memory of your eyes,
Your dull, stone eyes which haunt me in the dark.

Still Life

Moonlight Striking upon a Chess-Board

I am so aching to write
That I could make a song out of a chess-board
And rhyme the intrigues of knights and bishops
And the hollow fate of a checkmated king.
I might have been a queen, but I lack the proper century;
I might have been a poet, but where is the adventure to
      explode me into flame.
Cousin Moon, our kinship is curiously demonstrated,
For I, too, am a bright, cold corpse
Perpetually circling above a living world.

Poetic Justice

Double-flowering trees bear no fruit, they say,
And I have many blossoms,
With petals shrewdly whirled about an empty centre,
White as paper, falling at a whiff of wind.
But when they are gone
There are only green leaves to catch at the sunlight,
Green monotonous leaves
Which hide nothing.

To Francesca Braggiotti

After Seeing Her Dance: "Fragrance"

White—
As the dawn on white roses,
Bright—
As sunlight on your rope of roses;
As a feather tossed in the quick of the wind,
As a crystal figure swept by a rainbow rain.
Dancer of silver shadows,
You are all youth and freshness,
Like a sharp spear against ivy,
Like a bow pulled to quivering,
Like an arrow rushed from a shaking bow.
Your arms are gestures of a morning earth,
The arc of your leaping legs a shout of loveliness,
Your movements the shining silence of the on-coming
    sun.

You dance in the dawn,
You dance over green lawns in a leaf-rhythm,
Weaving patterns with your rope of roses,
Printing a white, fleeting pattern of yourself,
Of your bright body against sudden, startled green.

Dissonance

From my window I can see the moonlight stroking the
    smooth surface of the river.
The trees are silent, there is no wind.
Admirable pre-Raphaelite landscape,
Lightly touched with ebony and silver.
I alone am out of keeping:
An angry red gash
Proclaiming the restlessness
Of an incongruous century.

A Rainy Night

Shadows,
And white, moving light,
And the snap and sparkle of rain on the window,
An electric lamp in the street
Is swinging, tossing,
Making the rain-runnelled window-glass
Glitter and palpitate.
In its silver lustre
I can see the old four-post bed,
With the fringes and balls of its canopy.
You are lying beside me, waiting,
But I do not turn,
I am counting the folds of the canopy.
You are lying beside me, waiting,
But I do not turn.
In the silver light you would be too beautiful,
And there are ten pleats on this side of the bed canopy,
And ten on the other.

Amy Lowell was born on February 9, 1874, in Brookline, Massachusetts, the daughter of wealthy Bostonians. Her siblings included the astronomer Percival Lowell and Harvard University president Abbott Lawrence Lowell. She grew up at Sevenels, her father's ten-acre estate. She spent six months in Europe in 1896 and traveled up the Nile the following year. She purchased Sevenels after her father's death in 1900. Her first published poem appeared in the *Atlantic Monthly* in August 1910. She published her first book, *A Dome of Many-Coloured Glass*, in 1912. Visiting England in 1913 and again in 1914, she met H.D., Ford Madox Hueffer, and Ezra Pound, and contributed to the first anthology of Imagist poets, *Des Imagistes* (1914), although she soon split with Pound and Ford over the definition of Imagism. She edited the annual anthology *Some Imagist Poets* from 1915 to 1917. Her later poetry collections included *Sword Blades and Poppy Seed* (1914), *Men, Women and Ghosts* (1916), *Can Grande's Castle* (1918), *Pictures of the Floating World* (1919), and *Legends* (1921). She wrote two books of criticism, *Six French Poets* (1915) and *Tendencies in Modern American Poetry* (1917), and the biography *John Keats* (1925). Her translations of Chinese poems, prepared in collaboration with

Florence Ayscough, were published as *Fir-Flower Tablets* in 1921. She died of a stroke on May 12, 1925. The actress Ada Dwyer Russell, her companion since 1909, oversaw the post-humous publication of Lowell's work, including *What's O'Clock*, which won the Pulitzer Prize in 1926.

The texts of the poems in this volume are printed as they appeared in one of Amy Lowell's collections:

A Dome of Many-Coloured Glass (Boston: Houghton, Mifflin, 1912).

Sword Blades and Poppy Seed (New York: Macmillan, 1914).

Men, Women and Ghosts (New York: Macmillan, 1916).

Pictures of the Floating World (Boston: Houghton Mifflin, 1919).

Legends (Boston: Houghton Mifflin, 1921).

Fir-Flower Tablets: Poems Translated from the Chinese by Florence Asycough . . . English versions by Amy Lowell (Boston: Houghton Mifflin, 1921).

What's O'Clock (Boston: Houghton Mifflin, 1925). Lowell read proof for this edition, although it was not published until after her death. [Copyright © 1925 by Houghton Mifflin Company, renewed 1953 by Harvey H. Bundy and G. d'Andelot Belin, Jr., Trustees of the Estate of Amy Lowell. Reprinted by permission of Houghton Mifflin Company. All rights reserved.]

Except for "The Doll," which is taken from *East Wind* (Boston: Houghton Mifflin, 1926), and "A Rainy Night," taken

This volume presents the texts of the original printings chosen for inclusion here, but it does not attempt to reproduce nontextual features of their typographic design. The texts are presented without change, except for the correction of typographical errors. Spelling, punctuation, and capitalization are often expressive features and are not altered, even when inconsistent or irregular. The following typographical errors have been corrected (cited by page and line number): 8.23, pinacles; 108.6, It.

NOTES

1.3 Apples of Hesperides] Golden apples on a tree in a garden at the remote western edge of the world, protected by the Hesperides, identified in some versions of the myth as the daughters of Night and Erebus.

2.1 ΔΙΨΑ] Thirst.

3.20–21 Carpaccio's Picture / The Dream of St. Ursula] The painting is part of Vittore Carpaccio's cycle depicting the life of St. Ursula, now in the collection of the Accademia in Venice.

5.16 Crépuscule du matin] Morning twilight.

36.18 *épergnes*] Center dishes whose branches support smaller dishes.

48.15 *Ssŭ-ma Hsiang-ju*] Chinese poet (179–117 B.C.) noted for his work in the *fu* (rhyme-prose) genre.

51.8 Venus Transiens] The transit of Venus.

67.17 Maladie de l'Après-Midi] Afternoon illness.

72.16 *Andreas Zorn*] Swedish painter and etcher (1860–1920) noted particularly for his nudes.

80.3 "Faites vos jeux, Messieurs."] "Make your bets, gentlemen."

86.3–4 Minos and Dictynna] Minos, legendary king of Crete; Dictynna, Cretan nymph, an attendant of Artemis.

87.2   *FIR-FLOWER TABLETS*]   In her introduction to the book, Lowell writes: "Let me state at the outset that I know no Chinese. My duty in Mrs. Ayscough's and my joint collaboration has been to turn her literal translations into poems as near to the spirit of the originals as it was in my power to do."

87.4   *Li T'ai-po*]   Chinese poet (701–762) often known as Li Po.

92.5   *Tu Fu*]   Chinese poet (712–770).

107.9   Wimpole Street]   Elizabeth Barrett Browning lived for many years with her family at 50 Wimpole Street in London.

108.2   Casa Guidi]   Residence of Robert and Elizabeth Barrett Browning in Florence.

112.5   Nuit Blanche]   White night.

125.31   Moussorgski's "Pictures"]   Modest Mussorgsky's piano suite *Pictures at an Exhibition* (1874).

137.10   Francesca Braggiotti]   Italian dancer (1902–98) who later worked as a film actress.

INDEX OF TITLES
AND FIRST LINES

ABOUT THIS SERIES

The American Poets Project offers, for the first time in our history, a compact national library of American poetry. Selected and introduced by distinguished poets and scholars, elegant in design and textually authoritative, the series makes widely available the full scope of our poetic heritage.

For other titles in the American Poets Project, or for information on subscribing to the series, please visit: www.americanpoetsproject.org.

ABOUT THE PUBLISHER

The Library of America, a nonprofit publisher, is dedicated to preserving America's best and most significant writing in handsome, enduring volumes, featuring authoritative texts. For a free catalog, to subscribe to the series, or to learn how you can help support The Library's mission, please visit www.loa.org or write: The Library of America, 14 East 60th Street, New York, NY 10022.

AMERICAN POETS PROJECT